SMALL GROUPS
From Start to Finish >>

Doug Fields > Matt McGill

SMALL GROUPS
From Start to Finish >>

Why I love small groups!

Many people, both in and outside the church, live lonely, unconnected lives. They have developed the skill of navigating through life with weak and powerless relationships termed "friendships." Yet, within most of these friendships they remain strangers to their hopes, dreams, fears, and sin. Small groups are an answer to superficial living.

Today's teenager is a product of an unconnected generation of adults. Different than their parents, teenagers want to talk, connect, and live life together in authentic, life-changing ways. Small groups within a youth ministry are a method to combat the bigness and isolation of our culture.

I love getting my students in small groups!

In big groups...
Students can hide and relate in inauthentic ways.

In small groups...
Students can be known, loved, challenged, discipled, and cared for.

Before I used small groups in youth ministry, many students would slip through the cracks. I would feel guilty because I could disciple only a handful of students. I knew a lot of names, but I could know only a few students really well. Now, because of our small group structure, I am confident a student won't slip through the cracks when he/she is in a small group. I love ministering with this type of confidence.

I love watching my volunteers minister to students!

In big groups...
Adult volunteers can easily become "stand around" chaperones with little to do.

In small groups...
Adult volunteers can discover the joy of being a shepherd of students.

Before small groups, many volunteers would serve for short time periods because they felt like they weren't really contributing. If they weren't up front (e.g. teaching, skit, announcement, etc.), they didn't feel needed. Now, as small group leaders, they take the role of youth minister and make it their goal to disciple the few students entrusted to their care. Our volunteer turnover is minimal because they have become ministers (chaperones quit, ministers rarely do). I love ministering with the adults who have become long-term leaders.

I love growing big and small at the same time!

Youth ministries grow through small groups.

When students are cared for and challenged to grow in their faith, their spiritual growth causes numerical growth. Evangelism is a natural by-product of a life committed to Jesus.

When youth workers ask me, "How do I grow my group?" I respond by saying, "Care for the students God has entrusted to your care." Love them by getting them in a small group and aligning them with a caring adult leader.

I love sharing what I've learned with other youth workers!

This resource is a response to the hundreds of youth workers who have asked me, "Where do I start with small groups?" I didn't write it to convince you of the need for small groups; I'm assuming you have already decided the value of small groups.

The reason for this resource is to help you through the process of starting small groups and provide you with ideas that helped us during our small group journey.

This resource is divided into two parts. In part 1, you'll find a detailed 10-step process for creating a small group ministry from scratch and launching it at your church. In part 2, you'll find about 50 practical small group resources (99 pages) that we have used at Saddleback Church in our student ministry.

I love saving youth workers time!

Please feel free to use any of the resources on the CD ROM (that's why they are there). Take our name off, edit what you want, and don't worry about trying to "re-create the wheel". Actually, one of the favorite elements of putting this together was thinking about how much time this could save you. Also, check out the CD ROM to see some of the PowerPoint slides that we've created for you to use in getting the word out to your students. [Our only request at www.simplyyouthministry.com is that you don't publish our material or put it on the internet.]

As I try to save you time, move through this notebook slowly. Don't try to do it all in one day. If you do, you may get a shallow idea of small groups that won't last beyond your first wave of opposition. I like to tell youth workers that I can't show them how to build a ministry fast, but I can help them build health. Health takes time.

I love not knowing everything about youth ministry!
I started working with 7th grade boys when I was still a junior in high school in 1979. One truth I've learned about youth ministry in all those years is that I've got a lot to learn about youth ministry. As a youth pastor, I'm still in the trenches working full-time in the church and my learning cycle is always on "high". I want you to know that because I don't expect this to be a perfect document. I'm sure I've missed some ideas, principles, and steps in putting this together. This was written during some late-night sessions and I'm sure we've missed a few things and made some mistakes. Sorry...I'm still learning with you.

I love challenging my volunteers to take my title: Minister to Students

If an adult volunteer pours time, counsel, biblical teaching, and regular care into a student, he/she is playing the role of that student's youth minister. I challenge our small group leaders to act as ministers to the small group students under their care. At Saddleback Church, I have the title Minister to Students, but I'm happy for small group leaders to own that title when they care for students in their groups. When a student has a track meet, I'd rather the small group leader get an invitation than me as the youth pastor. I want the small group leader invited to the birthday parties, graduations, etc... If I challenge my leaders to take on the role of minister to their students, our youth ministry will grow. I can't care for very many students on my own.

As you read this letter from a former student, you'll see the pastoral influence her small group leader had in her life (to be honest, I don't even remember this girl). This summarizes what I'm try to get small group leaders to do.

Kathleen,

If I were giving a sermon right now, I would begin with prayer and thank God for the dedication you showed me in being my small group leader. I love telling people, "Kathleen is my small group leader—she's the best!" Next to God, you have had the greatest influence in my life. I want to grow up and love people like you, Jesus like you, my (future) husband like you do, and be a small group leader like you.

What's amazing about you is that all the girls in our small group felt like you liked them the most. We also felt your push. As I look back over my junior high and high school years, you loved me enough to challenge me to change. Thank you for always asking about my prayer life, my quiet times, my ministry, my heart for my lost friends, and to quote you, "My love for Jesus." Thank you for wanting to see me change.

I was talking to a friend at college and he said, "Kathleen sounds awesome. You should tell her what she meant to you." So, that's why I'm writing. I loved Saddleback's youth ministry, but if it wasn't for you and the small group, I don't know if I would have loved church, God, and others the way I did. There's a lot more to write, but I'll tell you in person next time I see you.

I love you,
Erika

This is a great example of why the youth minister doesn't need to try to minister to everyone.

I love working with my friend Matt McGill!

I've asked my friend Matt McGill to help me synthesize all that we've done at Saddleback Church and to find the resources we've used that might be helpful to you. Matt was in my small group when he was a teenager. Matt graduated from my youth ministry in 1991, went to college, and has been working with me at Saddleback Church since 1995. Today, he is the backbone behind our student ministry and runs everything when I'm not around (actually, even when I am around). He's one of the smartest humans I know, and I can't imagine doing youth ministry without him. Aside from this paragraph, Matt and I wrote every word together. It's our combined prayer that this resource helps you get students in small groups,

In the trenches with you,

Doug Fields & Matt McGill

Doug Fields is the Pastor to Students at Saddleback Church in Southern California. He has been in youth ministry since 1979 and has authored 30+ books and developed a youth ministry resource company (www.simplyyouthministry.com) to simplify youth ministry and save youth workers time. He and his wife Cathy have 3 children (one of which is a teenager in his youth group).

Matt McGill has been on staff since 1995 and has known Doug since he first came to Christ as a 9th grader in Doug's youth ministry. Matt is a thinker, a lover of God's Word, and a great youth worker. He loves to brag about his boys Max and Marc, and his wife Misha (who was in Doug's wife's small group as a teenager).

SMALL GROUPS
From Start to Finish >>

PART ONE > 10 Steps for Starting a Small Group Ministry

SMALL GROUPS
From Start to Finish >>

PHASE ONE > Laying the small group foundation

STEP 1 > **DREAM IT SMALL**
>> Take time to consider what small groups can do for your ministry

STEP 2 > **SUPPORT THE DREAM**
>> Start the necessary groundwork

STEP 3 > **DETERMINE THE DETAILS**
>> Identify some essentials for a smooth transition

STEP 4 > **CLARIFY YOUR GROUPINGS**
>> Divide your students into small groups

STEP 1 > DREAM IT SMALL

>> Take time to consider what small groups can do for your ministry

Get alone
Pray
Dare to dream
Begin with the end
Think through the basic questions

This is the step where you begin to dream about what you've already considered—small groups. This first step doesn't have any conventional rules to follow other than to follow no rules. I want to encourage you to begin the process by allowing your heart and mind to go for it. Experience the joy of playing the "what if" game as you think about what God could do through small groups to enhance the health of your youth ministry.

Get alone
Isolating yourself from distractions is very important. If you can, block out an entire day for this dream step. If you can't get away, unplug the phone and lock your door (and don't read your e-mail). If you don't have a whiteboard to capture your dream ideas, tape a long sheet of butcher paper to your wall to write notes on. Do this ahead of time so the search for office supplies won't be distracting.

Pray
The dream process is both enjoyable and dangerous. You probably know that you will take some heat for what you're dreaming about (beginning small groups). Some will berate you with comments like, "We've never done it that way," or "I'm going to leave the church if you cancel the Wednesday night program for small groups." Be in prayer and seek God's wisdom and direction before you take any major steps toward change. Ask him to purify your heart and clarify your dream.

This entire dreaming process needs to be a conversation between you and God. "God, make me passionate about what you want our students to experience in small groups. Open my eyes to how you want to move in this ministry..."

There's not a magic formula to this prayer time. Start by sacrificing your own desires and motives for God's direction. Use this time to be still, wait on him, and listen. As you dream, breathe in and out a simple prayer, "God, I need your wisdom and power... on my own, I can't do it."

Dare to dream

Dreaming the "what if" is an important and helpful exercise. I frequently do this for just about everything from planning a message to brainstorming an event. If you were to walk into my office right now, you would likely see some form of a dream sketched out on my whiteboard. (By the way, this notebook started as a dream on my whiteboard.)

It's fun to dream about what God can do if there is no risk or cost involved. Simply ask, "If I could do anything with small groups and I knew it would succeed, what would I do?"

As you dream about going small, dream big. Dream of resources you don't know how to get or can't afford. Dream of what it might be like if people asked to become small group leaders. Pretend that finding leaders isn't an issue and budgets are not a problem. Imagine that you have the best possible location(s) for small groups to meet. Dream! What could your small group structure look like?

As you dream, write your ideas on the whiteboard as fast as they arrive. Write irresponsibly. You may get an idea and think to yourself, "There's no way that can happen!" Write it anyway. If it costs too much, who cares? It's a dream. Write it down. It doesn't cost a cent to dream. You're on God's budget, his timing, and in his control. Allow yourself to spend some time seeing into God's infinite imagination.

Begin with the end

Because you are dreaming, you have the luxury of working backward. Start by visualizing the end result without worrying about how to get there.

During the dream process, try to capture a picture of what a student from a small group would "look like" five years after graduating from your ministry. Create a dream for how a small group will have impacted this student's spiritual life, family, friendships, ministry opportunities, and world view. Imagine what this student would be like if she had a God-fearing adult who invested in her life by caring for her, coaching her, and challenging her spiritual journey in a safe environment.

Capture the essence of the dream by writing a concise statement or bullet points that summarize your thoughts.

Here are some of my dream points:
- I want students to be known and cared for by other students and adults.
- I want students to form deep, authentic relationships with peers and adults.
- I want students to grow spiritually.
- I want students to learn what it means to follow Christ.
- I want students to explore God's Word together.
- I want students to see adults who love Jesus.
- I want students to view their small group leader as their youth pastor.
- I want students to consider their small group experience as a highlight and one of the best time investments of their week.

If you don't want to take the time to dream, you're moving too fast. Put this notebook down and take time to dream. Don't dampen your dreams by rushing to logistics. Allow your heart and ministry to be blessed by dreaming recklessly for a while. This notebook will be here when you're done dreaming.

Think through the basic questions
Once you've spent time dreaming the end product, it's important to begin thinking about the "how" of your small group strategy. Begin filling in the gaps from the ideal to the real before you get to Step 2. During the next step, you'll need to answer some basic questions for your critics and supporters. The answers to these questions will begin to formulate as you fill in the gaps.

If you need help, consider these questions:

- Why do I want small groups?
- What biblical purpose(s) will small groups serve (fellowship, discipleship, ministry, worship, evangelism)?
- How will students benefit?
- How will the youth ministry benefit?
- How will families benefit?
- Who would I like to use as small group leaders?
- Would I buy or write curriculum?
- When would I launch small groups?
- Should we meet in homes?
- Where will small groups meet?
- Will small groups be part of an existing program or will they replace a program?
- What day of the week?
- What time of day?
- What resources will I need?
- How many groups do we want to start with?

There are probably other questions that you'll need to answer. You don't need to take the time to answer them on the same day as your dream. They are just part of Step 1. This step may take one day or percolate for a year. Keep your questions in mind and write down your answers as they come to you.

When your dream develops some details, it's time to communicate it to a few carefully selected people. Gather your notes from this step, keep praying, and prepare to share what God has brought to your heart with others. The journey has begun.

CROSS REFERENCE > **STEP 1: DREAM IT SMALL**

>> If you want to read more information that might help you with this step, you can check out the pages in either Purpose Driven Youth Ministry (PDYM) or in Your First Two Years In Youth Ministry (FTY).

Get alone
FTY 73-77

Pray
PDYM 33-39, 345, 354-356
FTY 241

Dare to dream
FTY 23-26

Begin with the end
PDYM 137-151
FTY 86-89, 213-232

STEP 2 > SUPPORT THE DREAM

>> Start the necessary groundwork:

Decide if your dream is worth fighting for
Meet with key supporters
Seek input from your supervisor
Synthesize your learnings
Go one-on-one with your critics
Prepare for additional conflict

This step can be difficult because it will require leadership, and being a leader isn't always easy. Leaders come to understand that the majority of people hate change. You may get threats ("I'm leaving if you do this") and opposition ("That's a stupid idea") because you are trying to take the ministry into uncharted territory. Or, even worse, territory that has brought failure or pain in the past and has left residual feelings.

Youth ministry is not without risks. Consider a few ideas that may enhance a successful transition into small groups.

Decide if your dream is worth fighting for
One of the key considerations with any change is the energy it will require. If you and I were discussing this step, I would ask, "Are you willing to go to battle for small groups?" I would then ask, "Do you feel passionate enough about small groups that you're willing to keep going when it gets tough?" The answer to these questions need to be answered before moving on to Step 2.

Bottom line: expect personal attacks, challenges to your leadership style, or questions about your competence. I've experienced all three from students, parents, and church leaders (you should see my therapy bill). Even if the opposition is subtle, it will still feel like an uphill battle since most people hate change—even if it's in their best interest.

Fortunately, I have outlasted my critics and stuck to the dream I believe God birthed in me. The critics who eventually gave small groups a chance became deeper followers of Christ because of their experience. But what you're about to read and do isn't easy (actually, it's very easy to read...it's the doing that may result in tears).

Here are three "worst case" scenarios you may experience;
1. Some people may leave the church.
2. Some people will stay and complain (although they'll eventually stop).
3. Some people will try to run you out of the church.

If you don't believe that small groups are worth the effort, I'd suggest you go back to Step 1, and spend more time in prayer and dreaming. Or take some time to evaluate your leadership and determine if you can stomach the conflict. This move will require leadership, and if you're not willing to battle when it gets ugly, there's no use moving any further (since it may get ugly).

Meet with key supporters
Before sharing your dream with everyone, meet with a few key supporters of your ministry. Choose people who are supportive of your leadership and care about the health of the ministry. Since you know they have the best interest of your ministry at heart, challenge them to ask tough questions about your dream.

Key supporters may ask questions that you haven't thought of and highlight issues that could lead to trouble. They will also help you consider answers to problems you couldn't solve on your own. Sharing the dream with people you trust will be good practice for when you share it with your supervisor and others.

Simply arrange a one-hour meeting with you to share your heart and small group strategy (in that order). Answer big-picture questions with confidence, and show that you have thought through what you hope to accomplish. As you do, ask for their critical analysis of your dream.

It's okay if all of the details aren't in place because you are merely building support for your dream. Your goal is to prove that small groups are needed, your plan is feasible, you recognize your obstacles, and you have plans to deal with them. At the conclusion of this meeting, ask for their support ("Is this something you could get excited about? Can I plan on your support if we continue to move ahead?").

Seek input from your supervisor

After you have considered the input from the key supporters, pursue an opportunity to discuss small groups with your "boss." Don't rush to schedule this meeting—give yourself plenty of time to have thought through your feelings, your logic, and your strategy.

At the meeting, ask for two things: (1) Advice (in addition to getting useful input, asking for advice may help your supervisor to feel ownership in the idea of small groups), and (2) Public, verbal support (ideally from the pulpit).

If you don't get support from your supervisor, you may need to go back to Step 1 and rethink your dream. Because you and your ministry are under the authority of your supervisor, be sure to respect and honor the feedback he gives.

Synthesize your learnings

Compile the feedback from your key supporters and supervisor by asking yourself:
- What positive feedback did I get?
- What negative feedback did I get?
- What good ideas can I give them credit for?

Compile the answers and prepare to use them as support (or ammunition) when you approach your critics. Remember to continually pray for wisdom and pure motives as you move ahead.

TIP   >   GETTING UNDIVIDED ATTENTION

>> Only ask to meet with your supervisor for big changes (like moving toward small groups). By respecting your supervisor's time, you'll find a better chance of getting undivided attention when you need it most. <<

Go one-on-one with your critics

Now that you have great input from people who support you and from someone who can fire you (your supervisor), you can confidently share your idea one-on-one with those who may oppose change. Schedule short one-on-one meetings with the people who might try to dash this dream.

If you don't give your critics a forum to share their feelings with you, they will make one. They might talk about you and your plan behind your back or in meetings at inopportune times. I've found that taking this proactive step can neutralize the opposition and, in some cases, turn them into supporters. You will also discover that negative people usually aren't as opposed and reactionary to new ideas when you meet with them privately (as opposed to when you surprise them with an announcement in a group setting).

I've discovered that most negative people are insecure, critical, and often in need of more time and love than positive people. I'm not suggesting that all negative people will respond kindly to your changes, but they will appreciate the special attention and explanation (even if they don't tell you so).

TIP > **DEALING WITH COMPLAINTS**

>> What I have found in my ministry is that people complain about their passions. For instance, a person may complain that non-Christian students will not have a place to go if you replace your midweek program with small groups. You can redirect that complaint as a service opportunity by asking, "Can you help me think of a way to prevent that from happening? I would hate to see that happen, but I also know that small groups are the direction our ministry needs to go." If the person agrees to help, you have just recruited a volunteer who may help develop your evangelism strategy.

By the way, I don't believe you have to cancel a program to have small groups. I'll get into this later, but this is one of the oppositions I had when I made the transition from a midweek program to small groups. <<

In your conversation, you might say, "I know we've been on the opposite side of issues in the past, so I want to let you know of an experimental idea I'm working on. I want your input during the design phase." Your humble heart can soften a resistant attitude.

As you unfold your plan, give credit to your supervisor and other key supporters to show the critics that input was received and valued. By doing this, you will communicate that you're a team player and that you've got people who support your dream.

During your meeting(s) with the opposition, listen without interrupting and take notes. Don't become argumentative and risk turning the meeting adversarial. Instead, use this meeting to care for the person and graciously share your excitement for the support you've already received for a transition to a small group ministry.

Be appreciative of their time. There will be plenty of time to think through the comments, questions and objections at a later time. Before you end the meeting, pray together and ask for support.

Your opposition may not support your idea. No matter how hard you try, some people will simply refuse to budge because your ministry dreams represent change. Some would not support a new idea if the Lord Jesus presented the idea himself. While some people have hard-heart issues, this isn't always the case. The Body of Christ is diverse, and not everyone will agree to the same vision, priorities, and ministry methods. Don't take rejection personally.

TIP > KEEP FOCUS

>> Some people will try to drain you, control you, manipulate you, etc. It is important to keep focused on the end result of your dream. As you move forward, find ways to give credit to your opposition (as difficult as it may be). You want to value the input of others. The more you can make people feel appreciated, the more likely you'll earn their buy-in for future ideas without having to ask for it one-on-one. <<

Although, if you have a leader connected to your ministry who is consistently unsupportive your efforts to create small groups, you might consider transitioning this person out of your ministry. While this is never easy, I assure you it may be essential if you're going to launch your small group program. Paul saved his harshest rebukes for those who were divisive because he knew that ministry is hard enough without having conflict and resistance from within the Christian Camp. Proceed with gentleness, assure them it's not personal, and stand convinced of the necessity to make it happen.

Prepare for additional conflict
Once you put leadership behind your ideas and spend time with some key people, you are on your way to begin pursuing the details of a small group ministry. As you prepare to take the remaining steps, you will probably meet more conflict. People will talk to people and not articulate your dream with the same passion. This could result in a lot of questioning and doubt. When you share with supporters and critics, you can ask them to keep the small group talk confidential for a while, but word will begin to leak. Because of this, you will need to be ready to encounter more conflict.

You won't be able to anticipate and disarm everyone who will oppose small groups. Don't allow this to paralyze you. Be a leader and be prepared to move forward. Have your list of benefits memorized and confidently present them to those who oppose change.

When you have adequate support for your dream (not total support), it's time to begin the next step—determine the details. I know that the word "details" can be scary for the relational, outgoing, "what's-a-detail"-type of youth workers. I'm regularly scared... and if I could learn how to think through details (or find people who can), anyone can learn.

CROSS REFERENCE > **STEP 2: SUPPORT THE DREAM**

>> If you want to read more information that might help you with this step, you can check out the pages in either Purpose Driven Youth Ministry (PDYM) or in Your First Two Years In Youth Ministry (FTY).

Decide if it's worth fighting for
PDYM 344-345, 353
FTY 127-132

Meet with key supporters
PDYM 346, 65
FTY 244

Seek input from your supervisor
PDYM 346, 352, 65
FTY 156-164

Synthesize your learnings
FTY 239-252

Go one-on-one with your critics
PDYM 346-347
FTY 181-182, 249-250

Prepare for additional conflict
PDYM 347
FTY 127-146

STEP 3 > DETERMINE THE DETAILS

>> Identify some essentials for a smooth transition:

Determine your basic small group structure
Create a schedule for your small group program
Choose curriculum
Decide where small groups will meet
Be choosy about which homes you use
Think through the church building
Evaluate your program design against your dream
A closer look: Saddleback's Small Groups

In your meetings with supporters, your supervisor, and the opposition, hopefully you gleaned some insight to add shape to your dream. Now, use the insights you gained from your meetings to begin adding some "how" (structure) to your "what" (dream).

Determine your basic small group structure
At this point, you should begin to think about your potential small group structure. Let me suggest three types of small group formats you might consider:

1. Small groups that meet before/during/after a program
2. A stand-alone small group program
3. Small groups formed, at random, during an existing program

In the first option you may have a large group time of teaching and singing followed by small groups. In the second option, you may have individual small groups that meet on their own (without any large group interaction). The first two options offer consistency because the same students are in the same group being cared for by the same adult each week.

The third option places students in small groups at random times and with random people. For example, if you want students to discuss something you've taught, you might say, "Grab a few people next to you and talk about this for a few minutes." That's a random small group. It has little structure and probably won't offer much support and accountability to your students. However, it does provide a way to introduce students to the idea of small groups.

I've learned that not one structure will fit every church. I encourage you to pursue collaborative wisdom when trying to discern what type will fit your church setting. As you determine your structure, work to answer these two questions.

1. What will be the duration of small groups?
How long will your small groups meet for?
- 6 weeks
- Semester
- School year
- Will they continue during the summer?

Several factors can influence the decision for how long your small groups will meet (e.g. a year-round school calendar, availability of space, commitment from your volunteers, etc...)

2. Will the groups be open or closed groups?
A closed group doesn't allow new students to enter it after the small group begins. An open group remains open to anyone at any time. Your choice will depend on the nature or purpose you choose for them.

If you choose to use closed groups, you might want to start by giving them a short life cycle (e.g. 6 weeks). By doing this, your small groups can have the option of making a new commitment at the six-week

TIP > THE EXPERIMENTAL FACTOR

>> One benefit of starting with a 6-week plan is the experimental factor. I can get students and leaders to try anything for 6 weeks if I label it an experiment. You may tell them that at the end of six weeks, you'll re-evaluate the idea, make some adjustments, and either cancel small groups or strengthen them and continue. <<

mark. Closed groups and a short time frame have some advantages:

- By the end of the 6-week cycle, you'll know if you need to make a leadership adjustment.
- Students who joined your ministry during the 6 weeks don't have to wait too long before joining a new one (since there will be new groups starting every 6 weeks).
- Both students and leaders will be more likely to make a commitment to a closed group if it's a short time commitment.

Create a schedule for your small group program
Determine a practical itinerary that is simple and flexible. Every minute doesn't need to be structured, a loose schedule will help small group leaders manage their time and meet your expectations.

Choose curriculum
Curriculum should be easy to use and require minimal preparation time for your small group leaders. For many volunteers, it's difficult enough to carve out 2 hours a week for a small group, let alone spend another few hours preparing to teach complex curriculum. Eventually, they will become frustrated, burn out, and quit. I want curriculum that leaders can consume and facilitate with about an hour of preparation.

If you purchase curriculum, be sure to make adjustments to fit your students, church setting, and theology. A curriculum sold in bookstores won't be culturally relevant to every church context, so you'll want to adjust it to maximize its impact for your setting. Basically, you know your students better than the curriculum writer.

TIP > CREATIVE COLLABORATION

>> If you consider writing your own curriculum, gather volunteers to help you. When I write curriculum or prepare a message, I rarely do it without the input of others. I find that by using other people to create a think tank, I spend less time and effort. The end product is always better than if I did it myself. Also, this is a great way to train leaders to think critically as they make their own ministry decisions. <<

When using curriculum within small groups, I typically suggest having all the small groups use the same material. Here's a few advantages to this approach:

1. The ability to have the curriculum parallel another program (your mid-week small groups can discuss what you teach on Sunday morning).
2. Small group leaders can help each other since everyone is using the same curriculum.
3. You can easily monitor the depth and quality of teaching content.
4. You can create a comprehensive teaching plan for all your students.

This isn't "the" way to use curriculum, it's just the one that I'm most comfortable with. I know of several churches that allow each small group to choose their own curriculum. Do whatever fits for you.

Decide where small groups will meet
I'm sure you can think of many places for your small groups to meet: at schools, in parks, underground bunkers, aquariums, stables, hot air balloons, etc... For the sake of simplicity, I'm going to limit the options to either meeting in a home or at the church property.

TIP > **DOWNLOADABLE CURRICULUM**

>> Our curriculum (www.simplyyouthministry.com) is ready to edit and personalize. It comes in electronic format and can be easily adapted and edited to fit your needs. <<

If you choose to meet in homes, consider:

Good candidates for hosting small groups:
- Those who have committed to be small group leaders
- Students' homes
- Big homes
- People who understand and appreciate youth ministry
- People without white carpet
- People who don't fear messy students

Bad candidates for hosting small groups:
- Homes with priceless heirlooms scattered throughout the house
- Homes where furniture is covered in plastic
- Mean homeowners
- Homes with neighbors who complain frequently (too many cars on street, too much noise, etc...)
- People with several pets
- Young, single college guys' apartments
- Osama Bin Laden's bunker

Be choosy about which homes you use
If the family agrees to consider allowing their home to be used, ask whether you can come by to meet them (if you haven't), see their home, and ask questions. Try to take someone with you so you can compare notes once you leave. Before you visit the home, think through questions you'll need to have answered.
Here are some you may want to ask:

1. Can the family commit to the needed time frame (school year, 6 weeks, whatever you choose)?
2. Which room(s) in the house can be used?
3. How many students can comfortably occupy the available room(s)?
4. How many students can meet in the largest meeting room (if you decide to have several small groups meet in one house)?Don't ask them to commit, ask them to prayerfully consider allowing you to use their home. Tell them you're not 100% sure you'll need their home. This "flexible" language allows you to be discerning as you choose homes.

Don't ask them to commit, ask them to prayerfully consider allowing you to use their home. Tell them you're not 100% sure you'll need their home. This flexible language allows you to be discerning as you choose homes.

Don't settle for locations where there are lots of distractions (e.g., pets, small children, screaming husband watching sports, or nonunderstanding
siblings who come home and shout, "Who the *&#@!
parked in my spot?" Yes, that actually happened to us).

When visiting the home, pay close attention to atmosphere issues:
- Is there tension in the home?
- Did the phone ring a lot?
- Does the dog try to mount your leg?
- Are there ashtrays or alcohol containers present? (This may be a bonus for some denominations.)
- Is there a velvet painting of dogs playing poker?
- Could pets be put away during small group time?
- Is the house too nice or fragile?
- Is the house too messy and stinky?
- Is the house big enough?
- Do you trust the family?

Think through the church building
If you decide to use the church building for small groups, think carefully about specific meeting locations. You don't want students having to shout over choir rehearsals, creating a mess in the pastor's office, wrestling in the baptismal, etc. It's not a bad habit to evaluate the church facilities as you would a house.

TIP > **HOST HOME EXPECTATIONS**

>> If you decide to use the home, make sure your leaders know the expectations of the family. Explain any issues you noticed in the home and give ideas of how you might deal with them. <<

You may choose to use a combination of homes and church facilities. While most of our small groups meet in homes, some meet on our church property. A few affinity groups, who have been in trouble with the law, meet at the church because it makes better sense than having them meet in a home (where the small group members might see to it that the host family's prize-winning poodle is hopped up on crack).

Evaluate your program design against your dream

Step back from all of your planning and ask, "Is this how we want our small group program to look?" It is very easy to read this notebook and find yourself drifting off course from the original dream you felt led to follow. Before you move to the next step, take time to review the dream and compare it to what you have developed. It's okay to adjust it.

A closer look: Saddleback's Small Groups

I'm asked all the time about our small group program. While it's far from perfect, I'm happy to share with you what we do and use this to further illustrate this step. Here are some of the details of our small group programs:

Middle School Ministry (aka: Junior High)

Determine your basic small group structure

Our middle school small groups are a "stand alone" program (option 2 page 27).

Each group has anywhere from 4-10 students in the group and an adult leader (some have co-leaders).

What will be the duration of small groups?

The small groups meet once a week for the duration of the school year (and they take the summers off).

Will the groups be open or closed groups?

These middle school groups are closed groups. Same sex.

Create a schedule for your small group program
> 6:45 One small group leader arrives at host home
> 7:00 Students within this one small group arrive and hang out
> 7:15 Small group begins with students catching up on their week (share their highs and lows)
> 7:30 Interactive Bible study
> 8:00 Prayer requests and group prayer time
> 8:15 Parents begin to pick up students
> 8:45 Adult leader is the last to leave

Choose curriculum
There are two curriculum tracks, one each for 7th and 8th grades.

Decide where small groups will meet
Typically a single small group meets in a home.

Other: groupings
All small groups are divided by gender and grade. After that, each student is given the choice to prioritize the following criteria:
> --meeting day
> --near their home
> --friend: _____
> --people from their school
> --a special leader

This information is collected on a registration card throughout the summer months. Only registered students are assigned to a small group. Once registration closes, all of the students are assigned to groups according to gender, grade, and their chosen preference.

High School Ministry

Determine your basic small group structure
Our high school small groups meet within a program (option 1 page 27).

While the middle school has stand alone small groups, the high school ministry fills several homes (20+) with multiple small groups in each home. Anywhere from 3-10 small groups will meet in each home (each small group typically has anywhere from 5-10 students in it). Each house group begins with a large group teaching time (usually meeting in the living room) and then all the students break into their groups and find meeting places throughout the house (see schedule below).

What will be the duration of small groups?
The small groups meet once a week for the duration of the school year (and they take the summers off). Each group has anywhere from 4-10 students in the group and an adult leader (some have co-leaders).

Will the groups be open or closed groups?
These high school groups are open groups.

Create a schedule for your small group program

6:45 Several small group leaders arrive at host home
7:00 Students from the school arrive and hang out
7:20 All students meet in large room; teach lesson
7:45 Small groups break into meeting rooms throughout the house
  • Discuss how everybody is doing
  • Interactive discussion based on large room teaching
  • Pray for each other
8:45 Students gather informally to hang out
9:00 Everyone leaves; leaders make sure all students are gone before they leave

Choose curriculum
Every small group uses the same curriculum. Currently, we write all of our own curriculum.

Decide where small groups will meet
During the school year, our small groups meet in homes. During the summer, all the groups meet together (as a collective group) at the church property. We do this for three reasons:

  1. Students are taking vacations during the summer and attendance is very inconsistent.

2. We want to give our volunteer leaders a several-week break from their small group.
3. We want to give our host homes a break from having people in their home every week.

Location is an important consideration. When we first started meeting in homes, I wanted two host homes near the church property. Now, after several years and many host homes, I want the homes closer to the schools our students attend.

Other: groupings
The only consistency across all the high school small groups is that all groups are same-sex small groups. After that, I think we use every possible method for grouping students. The most common solution is by grade. Although a registration card is not required for high school (like it is for Junior High), we do encourage our students to fill them out. This gives us an idea of where to place leaders, provides an excuse to follow up with an invitation to join a small group, and have a suggestion of who to put in their group (we ask for the name of one friend). High school small groups are open, anyone is free to come and go (although we encourage consistency).

If you're not a detail-oriented, person this step may have brought some discomfort...sorry. But, if you want the best for your small groups, you will have to consider some important essentials that you skipped during the dream step. At this point in the process, you should have a lot of your ideas fleshed out for what your small groups will look like. You've got a lot more work to do, but at least you have an idea of what needs to happen. Now, you might be thinking, "Wait a minute, you haven't talked about grouping my students." You're right; this issue is so important, we've made it one of our ten steps...and it's the next one.

CROSS REFERENCE > **STEP 3: DETERMINE THE DETAILS**

>> If you want to read more information that might help you with this step, you can check out the pages in either Purpose Driven Youth Ministry (PDYM) or in Your First Two Years In Youth Ministry (FTY). Also, resources in Part 2 of this notebook that correspond with this step have resource titles listed below.

Determine your basic small group structure
PDYM 144-146

Create a schedule for your small group program
PDYM 152-154

Choose curriculum
PDYM 147

Decide where small groups will meet
PDYM 151-152

Evaluate your program design against your dream
FTY 272-273

A closer look: Saddleback's Small Groups
PDYM 152-154

>> **Related resources in Part 2:**

Choose curriculum
Sample Curriculum Leader Notes 84
Sample Curriculum Student Worksheet 92
Sample Teaching Plan 96,99
Curriculum Survey 101
Small Group Evaluation Guide 103
Considerations When Writing Curriculum 106
First Night Of Small Groups 108

STEP 4 > CLARIFY YOUR GROUPINGS

>> Divide your students into small groups:

Recognize the pain potential
Identify some grouping options: objective, subjective, or random
Choose the option(s) that work best for you
Group Small
Minimize the growing pains ahead of time

What is the best way to group students? This is a very common question and my personal nightmare. I hate grouping students into small groups. There is no "one way" to do it and I wish there was so I could say, "Look, there is only one way to do this, so shut up and like it." Oh well, instead of one way, consider some options.

Recognize the pain potential

When you introduce your small group program into your ministry, essentially you are trying to administrate relationships. This is not an easy task! Even under the best of circumstances, all relationships experience tensions and difficulties, and by breaking students into groups, you are creating the potential for conflict. Egos, insecurities, poor communication skills, and personality conflicts are bound to plague your efforts to connect students in meaningful relationships. This isn't a reason to stop; I just want to let you know that groupings won't be easy. Again, I hate this part of small groups. It makes me want to quit every year I do it. So, when you hate it, think of me (I hate it too).

Identify some grouping options: objective, subjective, or random

Objective groupings are based on known facts about your students:
- Grade
- Sex
- School
- School activities
- Available night of the week
- The first initial of a last name

Objective methods seem to work best for small groups that are just beginning.

Subjective groupings require you to make a judgment call about your students. Subjective groupings might include comments like:

- "Let's put these groups together according to friendships."
- "These particular students might fit well together."
- "Let's make sure to separate cliques."
- "Let's place a few 'mature' students with a few 'immature' students."
- "I'd like to make sure one 'extrovert' is in each small group."
- "Let's put the five best in my small group and the worst five in Andy's group... I'm hoping he'll quit."

If objective or subjective methods won't seem to work, use some random method (e.g., draw names out of a hat, let students choose their own group, etc.) and ask your students to commit for six weeks. After the six-week session, make adjustments as needed.

Choose the option(s) that work best for you
Once you've identified the different options for grouping your students, simply select the methods that will work best for your small group ministry. Remember to be flexible since no grouping solution will fit every youth ministry setting. No matter what system or set of rules you create, relationships cannot be administrated with 100% effectiveness. I find that we typically use a combination of all three options within our small group ministry.

TIP   >   SUBJECTIVE METHODS

>> Subjective methods are probably best for splitting groups that may get too large. Be sure to communicate to students that you will "launch" new groups when they grow too big. If students know the group may divide into multiple groups, there will be less pain when you have to create new groups from the original one.   <<

Group small
Don't allow your small groups to get too large. You'll have to determine your ideal size based on what you hope to accomplish through small groups. You will have to monitor this RUTHLESSLY, as neither your students nor leaders will want to split into new groups.

My rule of thumb is, "When in doubt, go small." A small group might include between 2-4 students with one (or two) caring adult leaders. Then, create a second group when it grows to 8 students. Split the leaders and allow each to start over with four students.

When you can, put a co-leader in each group so that when a new group needs to be formed, the students will already be familiar with the leader. This is ideal. In our ministry, it rarely happens. Actually, as I write this, I've got one small group with 17 students and 1 leader. (I should probably be out finding more leaders rather than putting this notebook together.)

Minimize the growing pains ahead of time
A big challenge that faces a growing small group ministry is what to do when a small group is no longer small. Once you've determined your ideal small group size, be sure to communicate it to your students and leaders. Let them know that when a small group gets too big, it loses it effectiveness.

Consider using the word "launch" instead of "split." Launch has a missions feel (we're starting new groups), while split has a negative feel. It's simply semantics, but one seems to be more positive than the other.

Congratulations! You've reached the end of Phase 1. Your dream is in place, you've built a foundation for your small group program, and hopefully you have a group of supporters who are helping you think through your program. With a lot of challenges behind you, you're about to move to the really hard work (I wish I was kidding). Now is the time to develop adult leaders. I'm confident you can move ahead with students leading the small groups, but I'm just as confident that they won't materialize to be as healthy as groups led by adults. Adults intersecting the lives of students is the backbone of any healthy youth ministry.

CROSS REFERENCE > STEP 4: CLARIFY YOUR GROUPINGS

>> If you want to read more information that might help you with this step, you can check out the pages in either Purpose Driven Youth Ministry (PDYM) or in Your First Two Years In Youth Ministry (FTY).

Recognize the pain potential
FTY 236-239

Identify some grouping options: objective, subjective, or random
PDYM 143-146

Choose the option(s) that work best for you
PDYM 143-146

SMALL GROUPS
From Start to Finish >>

PHASE TWO > Develop your small group leadership team

STEP 5 > **CREATE JOB DESCRIPTIONS FOR YOUR LEADERS**
>> Identify your expectations and put them in writing

STEP 6 > **IDENTIFY AND CONFIRM LEADERS**
>> You can't do it alone! Move the key players into position

STEP 7 > **PREPARE YOUR LEADERS FOR MINISTRY**
>> Communicate your expectations and train leaders

STEP 5 > **CREATE SMALL GROUP LEADER JOB DESCRIPTIONS**

>> Identify your expectations and put them in writing:

Summarize your dream: articulate what you want leaders to know
Clarify your expectations: specify what you want leaders to do
Prioritize spiritual growth: define who you want leaders to be

At this step, don't be too concerned about whom you will ask to be small group leaders, instead be thinking about what they should eventually know, do, and become. It is easier to recruit small group leaders when you know what you'll be asking of them.

This is a relatively simple step in terms of what needs to be done—write down your expectations. At the same time, this step can become complex if you have a lot of expectations. Either way, be ready to write everything down so that at the end of this step, you can take everything and put it in an orientation packet for your small group leaders.

Here are some leadership principles you may want to consider when creating a job description for your small group leaders...

Summarize your dream: articulate what you want leaders to know
As you begin to think about what it will take to get your leaders "up to speed" regarding the small groups, make sure they know and understand the "why" behind small groups. You don't need to share every detail from Step 1, but at least paint a general picture of your plans. When your leaders catch your vision, they will serve with greater passion and effectiveness.

When leaders grasp the "why" behind a program idea, the "how" becomes exciting and empowering. My suggestion is to take your bullet points and/or statement from Step 1 and write it out for all your leaders. This should be in a primary spot within your orientation packet as well as discussed at your leaders' meeting.

Clarify your expectations: specify what you want leaders to do
When I speak to youth workers I often ask the question, "If I could guarantee you new small group leaders right now, could you use them?" Of course they say yes. But the truth is that they are not ready for leaders if the new leaders can't be given a clear description of expectations. If small group leaders don't know what you expect from them, they won't be effective and they won't last.

You know why small groups exist, and you know what role you want your leaders to play. Now, articulate your reasons and put them in writing. By doing this, you'll set your leaders up for a more successful small group experience. You will also get a better return on your recruiting efforts. People are willing to follow when they're clearly led.

Be specific. Be clear. Take away the mystery. If you want small group leaders to write a letter to each student that misses a small group meeting, list it. When it's a specific request, it has the potential to become a dynamic expectation. For your convenience, we've given several examples of expectations in part 2 of this notebook.

Prioritize spiritual growth: define who you want leaders to be
I want my small group leaders to be people who love God and like students--in that order and with that emphasis on love/like. Small group leaders don't need to be perfect, but they should be growing spiritually. I want them to be men and women who make pursuing God a high priority.

Our volunteers are frequently told that a growing relationship with God and commitment to family are more important than their involvement in ministry. I regularly invite volunteers to take a season off from leading a small group if they are struggling with either of these commitments. I fully understand that if they take me up on this, I will need to find more leaders. But by making this statement, I'm also making a statement that I value their spiritual journey more than their ministry. God's work in them is more important than what God will do through them. If leaders of leaders don't place an emphasis on personal spirituality, we will wind up having teams of people who are activities directors (or chaperones) rather than spiritual leaders (or shepherds).

Once you have completed Step 5, you should have created enough material for a short orientation booklet (just a few pages) that you can use to train your small group leaders. This material should be simple and concise. However, it should be filled with enough content to equip your leaders to know what to expect and what's expected. By doing this, it will make it much easier for you to recruit new leaders, and that's the next step.

CROSS REFERENCE > **STEP 5: CREATE SMALL GROUP JOB DESCRIPTIONS**

>> If you want to read more information that might help you with this step, you can check out the pages in either Purpose Driven Youth Ministry (PDYM) or in Your First Two Years In Youth Ministry (FTY). Also, resources in Part 2 of this notebook that correspond with this step have resource titles listed below.

Summarize your dream: articulate what you want leaders to know
PDYM 298-302

Clarify your expectations: specify what you want leaders to do
PDYM 301-302

Prioritize spiritual growth: define who you want leaders to be
FTY 65-68

>> **Related resources in Part 2**

Small Group Leader Orientation Booklet 161
Small Group Coach Orientation Booklet 174
Small Group Division Leader Orientation Booklet 178
Small Group Quick Reference Card 180

STEP SIX > Identify and Confirm Leaders

STEP 6 > IDENTIFY AND CONFIRM LEADERS

>> You can't do it alone! Move the key players into position:

Make the need known
Look within
Look outside
Keep looking
Compile names
Master the ask
Use "potential" language
Confirm new leaders

God didn't intend for your ministry to be a one-person show. Everyone is limited in how many meaningful relationships they can have with students. If your youth ministry is going to grow, you're going to need others to help carry the load and connect with those you can't minister to on your own. The goal for this step is to identify potential leaders and get some of them to commit to your small group ministry.

Make the need known
Many people in the church have a desire to serve—often, they just can't discern where their help is needed. It's easy for people to assume they aren't needed or quickly dismiss the idea of working with teenagers because of fear. I regularly get sad thinking of the untapped potential sitting in my church.

To identify leaders, you'll need to do whatever it takes to raise your congregation's awareness of your need for small group leaders. Don't think that your pastor or others will champion your announcement. You will become the primary voice behind your need.

As you get the word out, be sure to...
- Highlight the need students have for godly, caring adults in their life.
- Focus on how rewarding being a small group leader will be for the adults who serve.

Looking within

Looking within refers to those in your inner circle of relationships and influence. Launching small groups will make a huge impact on the health of your ministry, and you should be talking about the exciting changes that are coming soon. Every Christian you know can be a potential small group leader.

Often, youth workers overlook the people they know. I've learned that new programs can spark fresh desires among "old" bystanders. Because of this, talk to adults who occasionally volunteer to chaperone an event and cast the vision of them to become a small group shepherd instead. Approach parents you know, older siblings, and people already serving in other ministries (I know that sounds bad, but some people are looking for the opportunity to change ministries and they just need to be invited). As you look within, ask everyone you have a relationship with to be on the lookout for potential leaders.

Look outside

Look outside those you already know as potential candidates for small group leaders. Look beyond the typical types of people that you regularly identify with. You will need all types of personalities to connect with students of differing personalities (not multiple personalities). Normally, we look for people like us, and this limited approach can have a crippling affect on your ministry.

Look outside the common stereotype of a youth worker (e.g. young, lots of free time, relevant, high energy, extroverts, etc.) Some of my best small group leaders don't fit the mold of the stereotypical youth worker. In fact, several of our small group leaders are older than the students' parents. Teenagers need adults who will commit to care for them, not people who try to imitate their culture. When it comes to age, I'd rather have an older youth worker than a younger one.

Other "outside" considerations:
- You'll want some leaders to have had some "been there" life experience. If all the adults have lived a clean, pain-free life, they can care, but not share from their pain experience. Those who have had their share of pain can relate to hurt and better coach/guide/lead students during their pain.

• Ask your students which adults they believe would make good leaders for the youth ministry. Students watch adults and will know which ones like teenagers (you'll need to discern whether they love God).

Keep looking

Building your small group leadership team will never end. The healthier your leaders are, the deeper your students will grow. And when they grow spiritually, they'll develop a heart for evangelism, and they'll bring friends. This addition of more students will lead to the need for more leaders (it's a vicious, but wonderful, cycle). There's a lot to be done! Don't get discouraged, remember that God loves the students more than you do and he'll provide shepherds for sheep he has entrusted to your care.

17 Ways to Find Volunteer Youth Workers

1. Ask students whom they like.

2. Ask parents whom they trust.

3. Ask existing youth leaders whom they know.

4. Ask the pastor whom he sees an emerging leader.

5. Go to colleges and seminaries at the beginning of the school year to get unconnected students involved in your ministry.

6. Check the church directory and call someone who looks like the type of youth worker you need. (And since there is no specific look, anyone could fit. Just say, "I was looking through the directory, and you look like you'd be a great youth worker!")

7. Check out local parachurch organizations (Young Life, Youth for Christ, et cetera) to see whether any of their leaders aren't plugged into a church body.

8. Use parents.

9. Look within your own youth ministry. Have mature high school seniors work with junior high students or college students work with high schoolers.

10. Challenge newly married couples to start marriage by ministering together.

11. Make a request at the church membership class.

12. Find the sports coaches who attend your church. Many coaches are good with kids.

13. Write a letter to your congregation requesting assistance.

14. Ask some children's workers whether they might "graduate" with some of the their students to join your junior high team.

15. When you have the opportunity to speak to classes or other church groups (singles, couples, seniors) tell them you're looking for introverts. Many introverts don't think they make good youth workers because they're not wild and crazy. But they make great youth workers because they talk with students and go deep with them. While the extrovert runs around and says hi to everyone, the introvert engages students.

16. When you have the opportunity to speak to classes or other church groups (singles, couples, seniors), ask listeners to raise their hands if they grew up in a youth group and had a good experience. Seek them out. One of the reasons they had a good experience was because of caring leaders. Now it's pay back time for their good experiences by becoming leaders in your youth ministry. These people are usually warm to the idea of youth ministry.

17. Look for people who are tired of singing in the church choir.

Compile names

Consider keeping a simple contact list of all the people who are even remotely interested in serving as a small group leader. When you look in a variety of different places for new leaders (look outside), be sure to track names so you can approach them for a commitment at a later time.

Master the ask

While it may be okay to put an announcement in the church bulletin, you probably won't get a strong response. People have the heart to serve, but I've found that they typically need a nudge or invitation before they'll get involved. Promotion is good (ads, bulletin inserts, etc.), but personal invitations are better.

Most people serve because you value them enough to look them in the eyes and offer them an opportunity to take part in something bigger than themselves. There is power in asking, but to ask effectively—

- You've got to ask! I'd hate to miss the obvious.
- You've got to ask clearly. Get to the point.
- You've got to ask specifically. Don't mislead or manipulate.
- You've got to ask expectantly. Be shocked by a "no."
- You've got to ask persistently. ("No" might really be "not now," so ask again in a month or two—especially a strong candidate.
- You've got to ask creatively. Don't be afraid to use those who can only serve for a season (say, the summer) to help with projects.
- You've got to ask graciously. Leave a positive impression.
- You've got to ask prayerfully. See Matthew 9:37-38.
- You've got to ask confidently. Since you're not desperate, don't whine, beg, or create guilt. Don't be ashamed.

When I train youth workers, I ask a dozen people to stand up. Then, one by one, I ask, "How did you get into youth ministry?" The most common responses are—

I was asked by someone.
I felt God's call.

It seems obvious: you've got to look for people you can ask. Those who are called by God are going to hunt you down for an opportunity to join your team, but the remaining individuals are waiting for you to ask. (FTY pg. 187-188)

Don't limit your recruiting attempts to ads in the church bulletin. Most people look at requests like that and think, "That's too bad that the students need leaders. I'm sure someone will respond." Bulletins can spark interest in your need, but they won't have the power of asking in person.

Use "potential" language

As you cast a wide net to "catch" leaders for your ministry, don't make any hasty promises about leading a small group. When a person shows interest, you still need to be choosy—in fact, you should be picky. Don't ask out of desperation. It might feel like the right attitude to have, but moving too quickly can bring the wrong people into your ministry. I've learned the hard way that it's easier to "acquire" someone than "fire" them. Because of this, keep using the term "potential" with them until you're ready to confirm them and give them a small group. By doing this, everyone can be a potential leader until they're confirmed through your leadership process.

Confirm new leaders

When you raise the standard of the type of person you're looking for, you'll most likely find a higher quality of adult volunteer. But before you quickly say yes to those you have identified, you will want to take these potential leaders through some type of screening process before you confirm their small group leader role. You might want to consider asking (and expecting) potential small group leaders to:

- Fill out a ministry application;
- Provide a few references;
- Interview with you or a veteran small group leader.

Although it makes me sad to encourage you to be careful, it's simply a reflection of today's culture and therefore a reality. If you've been in ministry more than a year, you've most likely heard of someone "everyone trusted" who had a moral failure. When this happens, it can result in a loss of credibility and financial consequences for the church. When an adult has an inappropriate relationship with a student, it leads to emotional, physical, and spiritual consequences – it can (and usually does) devastate a youth group. You can't stop every sick person from their acts of evil, but you can have a standard that shields questionable people from becoming small group leaders.

Fill out a ministry application
When talking to a potential leader, I try to communicate my excitement for God blessing this person's desire to serve in our youth ministry. During this expression of excitement, I confidentially explain that volunteer leaders fill out a short application and go through an interview prior to becoming a small group leader. This application provides us with basic information and helps identify 'get to know you' questions. Years ago, this idea was mocked, but today, most church insurance companies require some type of screening process for adults who work with those under the age of 18.

Provide a few references
In addition to the application, we provide three reference forms and ask the applicant to give them to people who would recommend them working with students. If you choose to do this, you may want to specify the types of references you're looking for so you can draw more accurate conclusions about the person's character (e.g., give them to a church member and/or pastor, a family member, and employer).

TIP > **BACKGROUND CHECKS**

>> Currently, our church insurance provider requires us to do background checks. If you need to do them at your church, ask your local police department the legal way to do it. If there is a cost involved, get approval from your church (if needed) to cover the cost. <<

The references help us identify how the applicant is perceived. Spiritually mature? Relates well to others? Dependable? Etcetera. We ask that the forms come directly back to the church so they can remain confidential.

Interview with you or a veteran leader
Before scheduling an interview with a potential volunteer, read the completed application and reference forms and look for any potential "red flags." These flags can become helpful questions during the interview.

Red flags to look for are:
- Questions left unanswered on the application or reference forms
- Less than 3 reference forms returned
- Negative information on the application or reference forms
- New to the community with no previous church references
- New Christian (less than one year)
- Notations of mental instability
- Unreported information about felonies/convictions discovered from the background check (see tip)
- Unsupportive spouse
- Overly committed to other activities

The interview also allows potential volunteers to ask clarifying questions about the small group leader role. During the interview, I try to determine if they are a match for the youth ministry and a fit for leading a small group.

If you go this route, try to get the applicant to do most of the talking. Ask open-ended questions to draw out information. Questions that can be answered yes or no should be avoided. For example: a bad question is, "Are you excited about becoming a small group leader?" A better question would be, "Why do you want to be a small group leader?" Unfortunately, the process of finding leaders never ends. You will always need to integrate new people into your ministry. Small groups tend to be a common denominator with youth ministry growth.

Students who are cared for become healthy students, and healthy students invite their friends.

While the leadership process never ends, it does become more natural and part of the flow of your life—don't lose hope! Identifying and confirming leaders isn't easy for anyone I've ever met. You're not alone. Consider your ministry from God's perspective: he's more concerned for it than you are...you do the possible and he'll do the impossible and bring you leaders. When you get leaders, you'll need to love them and train them. That's the next step (and a lot more fun than Step 2).

TIP > HELP PREVENT PROBLEMS

>> You may get opposition from church members when you ask them to complete an application, provide references, and schedule an interview. When this happens, communicate the need for students' safety. Explain that this will become a standard process for those who volunteer. Tell them that by filling out the application, they are helping to prevent future problems. Also, if people aren't willing to invest time for this application process, that may be an indication of what they'll be like if they join your team. <<

TIP > ASK FOR A COMMITMENT

>> Since small groups are likely to be a major element of your ministry, consider raising the bar by asking for a commitment to a determined time frame. Students have too many adults coming in and out of their lives. Students need leaders who can be trusted to stay with them for a while. While you don't want leaders to feel trapped in your ministry, you do want to ensure a commitment. In our ministry, we ask for a 1-year commitment (or at least for a full school year). A commitment form conveys that we respect their future role as a small group leader. And their signature communicates they understand the commitment requested. For an example of our commitment sheet, see FTY page 279. <<

CROSS REFERENCE > **STEP 6: CREATE JOB DESCRIPTIONS FOR LEADERS**

>> If you want to read more information that might help you with this step, you can check out the pages in either Purpose Driven Youth Ministry (PDYM) or in Your First Two Years In Youth Ministry (FTY).

Make the need known
PDYM 282-289
FTY 185

Look within
PDYM 282

Look outside
PDYM 284

Keep looking
PDYM 284
FTY 186

Master the ask
PDYM 285-288
FTY 185

Use "potential" language
PDYM 288, 290-298
FTY 180, 184

Confirm new leaders
PDYM 296-297

STEP 7 > PREPARE YOUR LEADERSHIP TEAM FOR SUCCESS

>> Communicate your expectations and train leaders:

Keep your training brief
Disarm leaders' natural insecurities
Help leaders with tough stuff

Keep your training brief

You can't cover everything it will take to be a good small group leader at one meeting. Even if you try to cover a lot of details, the mind can only absorb what the seat can endure. Besides, the best small group leader training will come from the experiences of actually leading or co-leading a small group. Provide bite-sized training tips and allow some veteran leaders to share from their experience.

For instance, at your first meeting:

- Express your thankfulness for their commitment
- Summarize your dream: articulate what you want leaders to know
- Clarify your expectations: specify what you want leaders to do
- Prioritize spiritual growth: define who you want leaders to be

Keep from overwhelming your leaders, but give them enough training to get them started.

Disarm leaders' natural insecurities

If you're a veteran small group leader, you may have forgotten how difficult leading a small group can be. If so, you'll want to make sure that your new leaders understand how badly students need caring adults in their lives. Prepare them for students' lack of appreciation and attention and caution them about the sarcastic and insulting words they may hear on a regular basis.

New leaders should not feel like they have to be perfect. Many insecurities will arise and can move leaders to want to mask their imperfections. Help them to see that being real will speak volumes to students because many of them are hypersensitive to their own insecurities and failings.

Help leaders with tough stuff

Although there are probably dozens of difficult issues facing small group leaders, over the years it seems that the topics of confidentiality and discipline cause more questions than any others.

What to keep confidential

Leaders will be asked by students, "If I tell you something, do you promise to keep it a secret?" Please don't say, "Yes." The correct answer is, "I can't promise that I'll keep it secret. If what you tell me is about you getting hurt or abused, I can't be silent. If you're endangering yourself or someone else, I will tell someone. However, please know that I love you and will love you through the tough times. And I'll help you with whatever you're going through. Other than that, I will keep whatever you tell me between the two of us."

Leaders will need to know how to handle reportable information. Here's what I'd do; in cases of physical or sexual abuse that is imminent (that is, the student is in danger if she goes home tonight), I tell them to call 911, then call me. If the abuse happened in the past, notify me and together we'll make an appointment with Child Protective Services. In cases of threats of personal injury, call me, then we'll both contact the parents. In cases of others threatening to harm themselves, call me, then we'll talk with the student's parents.

Even if leaders believe the student isn't being truthful, I'd rather err on the side of caution. My small group leaders are not responsible for considering whether or not information is accurate. Their job is to report information about students who may be at risk. If it isn't true, the student learned a lesson about the seriousness of making such claims. If it is true, you've done the student an enormous favor by intervening.

Disciplining Effectively

Here is a picture of discipline:

Remember that in a race everyone runs, but only one person gets the prize. You also must run in such a way that you will win. All athletes practice strict self-control. They do it to win a prize that will fade away, but we do it for an eternal prize. So I run straight to the goal with purpose in every step. I am not like a boxer who misses his punches. I discipline my body like an athlete, training it to do what it should. Otherwise, I fear that after preaching to others I myself might be disqualified. 1 Corinthians 9:24-27

Here is a picture of punishment:

"...You weren't lying to us but to God." As soon as Ananias heard these words, he fell to the floor and died. Everyone who heard about it was terrified. Acts 5:4-5

I don't want students dying at youth group, but I do want to discipline them when necessary. Actually, discipline is a form of discipleship. For this reason, we need to train leaders to handle problems with wisdom. We need to show them how to love students both by example and by talking through tough hypothetical situations. At volunteer meetings, allow small group leaders to openly talk about tough issues in small groups. Give them specific examples to discuss...

TIP > PREPARED LEADERS

>> Prepared leaders will be long term leaders. In today's world of sexual misconduct accusations (false and true), it is important to protect your leaders, students, and your church. You can do this by encouraging same-sex relationships. Ideally your leaders will not spend much time alone with any one student. If a student needs to spend one-on-one time with an adult, it is important that the leader be the same gender of the student. Double check this with your supervisor. <<

- Johnny is always too affectionate with Erika and it makes others feel uncomfortable;
- Alex always asks questions that he knows the answers to;
- Rachel is easily offended and storms out in a rage regularly;
- Rebecca usually offends Rachel and causes her to storm out.

When you get your leaders talking though solutions to these types of problems, they begin to help each other see different options that weren't obvious in the moment. What could have been a punishment scenario now has the potential to be an opportunity for discipline and/or discipleship.

Everything that happens within your ministry will rise and fall with the quality of the leadership serving in your ministry. Training is important, but it is not the most important thing. Jesus gave very practical advice to his leadership "team"...

"Your love for one another will prove to the world that you are my disciples." John 13:35 NLT

Skills are important, but the Holy Spirit can work through the unskilled. Our primary responsibility as leaders is to worship God and maintain a passionate and authentic heart before him. New leaders must understand that their service in youth ministry isn't about building numbers and expressing their skills, it's about worship.

TIP > **MELLOW OUT**

>> Train your leaders not to get stressed out about little issues. Save discipline for big problems. There's too much little stuff happening all the time. Leaders will burn out if they focus on the little stuff. <<

CROSS REFERENCE   >   STEP 7: PREPARE YOUR LEADERSHIP TEAM FOR SUCCESS

>> If you want to read more information that might help you with this step, you can check out the pages in either Purpose Driven Youth Ministry (PDYM) or in Your First Two Years In Youth Ministry (FTY).

Keep your training brief
PDYM 307-309

Disarm leaders' natural insecurities
PDYM 275-277

Effective discipline
PDYM 327-343

SMALL GROUPS
From Start to Finish >>

STEP 8 > **GET THE WORD OUT**
>> Promote small groups to your students

STEP 9 > **FINALIZE ADMINISTRATIVE DETAILS AND GO**
>> Reexamine the essentials

STEP 10 > **MAINTAIN, EVALUATE AND LEAD**
>> Continue training, evaluate everything, troubleshoot problems, make adjustments

STEP 8 > GET THE WORD OUT

>> Promote small groups to your students:

Identify every promotional option available to you
Meet with parents
Maximize natural transitions
Ask students to sign up
Recognize some basic principles of promotion

Your dream is dreamt. The questions are answered (hopefully). Your leaders are confirmed. Congratulations! It's time to tell your world about the small groups you've been praying about and planning for. If you don't let students know what they are, when they begin, and where they meet, you may need to change the name from "small groups" to "tiny groups."

Identify every promotional option available to you
I'm not an expert in marketing, but chances are someone in your church has a lot of experience and can help you develop ways to get the word out to your church, parents, and students. I have learned that it's helpful to pursue multiple avenues of promotion.

Promotional ideas are filling your mailbox daily. Get in the habit of saving the ad campaigns that really catch your eye. Keep a file of these so you always have many ideas and options to choose from.

Here are some simple and common options:

1. Create a one page promotional piece that explains the why, when, and where of your small groups. The goal is to get students to see how small groups will help them connect with other students, grow spiritually, have a great time, and develop a relationship with caring adults.

Here are two sample tag-lines you might use:
   • When you're ready to take friendships and your faith to a deeper level, you're ready to join a small group.

   • Don't live life on the surface...go deeper...join a small group.

2. Mail out your brochure and have it available at all your youth ministry programs.

3. E-mail your students on a weekly basis and show the benefits.

4. Have your leaders (students and adults) make phone calls and invite unconnected students.

5. Have a student in your group create a small group webpage.

6. Have maps available to all your small group locations.

7. Make a video to show what small groups will look like. What will happen when students arrive? Show the benefits and details of how students will enjoy small groups. Or, make a humorous video that dispels myths about what will happen if they join a small group (e.g., you won't be tortured by the head of the house, run over by the teenager who has her driver's permit, bitten by the family dog, trapped in the basement, etc.)

8. Don't underestimate word of mouth. Get your leaders and key students talking about small groups like you would do with any big youth event (e.g., camp, concert, etc.).

9. Have testimonies from students who have been in small groups (if you don't have any from your church, get a student testimony from another church).

TIP > CHECK DRIVING DIRECTIONS

>> Check the accuracy of your maps. Use the exact map you intend to distribute. Driving mistakes lead to frustrated parents and disappointed students. For people who may already be uneasy with your new program, bad directions will make them angry. <<

10. Make power-point slides and have them showing while students enter your youth ministry programs. (Be sure to check out the several samples that we've included on the CD-ROM that accompanies this notebook.)

Meet with parents
Contrary to popular opinion, parents still have influence over their children. A parents' meeting is a great way to inform parents of your small group details. Don't rely on parents getting accurate information from their kids. A meeting will give you a chance to promote your program and allow them an opportunity to get all their questions answered.

Maximize natural transitions
How will students transition into small groups? Besides your initial kick-off, there will be natural times for you to easily transition students into small groups. Some of those entry points are:

Graduation: This is a time when students are primed for huge changes in their lives. Committing to a small group can be invaluable for surviving tough seasons of transition.

New Believers: Funnel the excitement and passion of new Christians by encouraging them to commit to a small group. Their small group involvement will build their faith.

TIP > **COLLECT MARKETING IDEAS**

>> Obviously, check the Internet as a source for marketing ideas (see free marketing ideas that you can subscribe to at www.emazing.com). Also, I get inspirational ideas from www.coolhomepages.com. While I don't endorse the content of these sites, they often inspire my creativity. <<

Spiritual growth commitment: When students make a commitment to renew their faith, encourage them to get connected to a small group.

Relocation: Make sure visitors hear about your small groups so they can meet people and make new friends.

Camps, retreats, special events, etc.: Few activities will build a wave of excitement in your ministry like a camp or retreat. Help your students by challenging them to maintain the camp momentum by joining a small group before the camp is finished.

Ask students to sign up

Consider having students sign up for small groups. This action will make follow-up a lot easier and take some of the guesswork out of who will/ won't attend.

Use the card to identify students' level of small group interest. Ask that every student in your group fill out the card and check the sentence that best describes them (request that they do this even if they don't want to be in a small group).

- Sign me up for a small group.
- I'm not sure; send some small group information to me.
- I'm not interested in small groups. Don't bug me. I don't like people.
- I'd like to, but I'm too busy. I can't be involved in one right now.

I've found that I can get just about everyone to fill out a card when I provide options that everyone could choose from.

Once you have a student signed up, a simple phone call will reinforce your excitement and remind them of their commitment. You could say something like, "We got the card you filled out last weekend and wanted to invite you to the new small groups starting September 1...."

Recognize some basic principles of promotion
I have some "rules" that I try to keep in mind when preparing promotional pieces. They might be helpful to you...

Concise: too many words are wasted words.

Clean: I'd rather it have a clean look versus a cluttered look.

Clear: when you have a choice between clear and cute, choose clear. Youth workers love to be creative, but when students have to decipher your message, you've just minimized the power of your promotion.

Professional: this is a personal bias, but when I use a promotional piece, I want it to look nice and be error-free since it is representative of our ministry. People are placing judgment on our ministry, and something as simple as a flyer can convey a quality (or lack thereof) of our ministry.

Once you have firmly embedded small groups into the culture of your youth ministry, you'll want to continue your promotional efforts. Students will need constant reminders about small groups since they are wonderful at forgetting things—especially important things. So, promote big before the group begins and continue to get the word out once they've started. I like thinking of promotional ideas a lot more than details... but that's the next step - one last look at the essentials.

CROSS REFERENCE > **STEP 8: GET THE WORD OUT**

>> If you want to read more information that might help you with this step, you can check out the pages in either Purpose Driven Youth Ministry (PDYM) or in Your First Two Years In Youth Ministry (FTY). Also, resources in Part 2 of this notebook that correspond with this step have resource titles listed below.

Identify every promotional option available to you
Meet with parents
Maximize natural transitions
Ask students to sign up
Recognize some basic principles of promotion
PDYM 256-258
FTY 109-111

>> **Related resources in Part 2:**

Identify every promotional option available to you
Letter to Small Group Students Interested in the H.A.B.I.T.S. 134
Letter to Students Interested in Small Groups 136
Small Group Church Bulletin Copy 145
Small Group Church Bulletin Copy (2) 146

Ask students to sign up
Small Group Registration Card 144

Recognize some basic principles of promotion
Weekend Message about Small Groups 139
Weekend Message about Small Groups (#2) 141

STEP 9 > FINALIZE ADMINISTRATIVE DETAILS AND GO!

>> Reexamine the essentials:

Double check all the details

When I mention the word "administration" to youth workers, I see a variety of responses:

- Some immediately move to an incoherent speech pattern.
- Some lose control of their face and instantly descend into sporadic twitching motions.
- Many run to the corner of the room, slam their eyes shut, and cry out repeatedly for a happy place.
- A few lose their appetite for days and wonder at the injustice of the organized world.
- But a select few, the true chosen ones of the Lord, will think, "Oh sweet, let's make something happen."

As we look at Step 9, it's easy to divide youth workers into one of two categories: those who will love this step (Matt), and those who will hate it (Doug). For those who "hate" details, this step will ensure that you don't forget the important stuff. Those who love administrative details have already made their own checklist and they can't wait to see what I've forgotten to include.

Double check all the details
A week or two before you launch your small group program, double check the details. This step is really a summary of everything we've talked about so far. Here are some checklist items to help you think through everything. Since I don't know everything about your ministry context, I can't guarantee I know everything that your small group program will require (so use the following list as a starting place to create your own list).

☐ **Small Group Dream Statement (Step 1)**
Have you clearly articulated why your small group program exists and what you hope it will accomplish? This statement will not only keep you on track, but it will also assist your leaders. This will serve as the foundation that supports your small group structure and everything else will try to reflect the statement.

☐ **Connect with key leaders for input (Step 2)**
Even though you are the lead youth worker and probably have some great ideas, don't miss the valuable input others can offer. Meet with them again to see if they still have questions and/or ideas that may be helpful.

☐ **Meet with supervisor for input and support (Step 2)**
Have you kept him/her informed of the details? Is there anything else you need from this person? Supervisors would rather be kept in the light than tripped up in the dark.

☐ **Meet with potentially negative people who might undermine your efforts to create a small group program (Step 2)**
Remember, if you don't solicit their input and support, your small groups could fall victim to criticism and prevent your dream from becoming reality.

☐ **Small Group Program Schedule (Step 3)**
Review your schedule for a typical meeting to make sure it will fulfill the dreams and expectations you have for your small group program.

☐ **Meeting place(s) confirmed (Step 3)**
If your groups are meeting in homes, make sure each leader and host knows what is expected of them and what to do should problems arise.

☐ **Students: placed into small groups (Step 4)**
Reconfirm the placement of your students into small groups based on the grouping style you chose during Step 4. Be sure to keep small groups small.

☐ **Leaders: confirm their commitment (Step 5-6-7)**
Make sure your leaders commit to spiritual, lifestyle, and timeframe expectations by getting them to sign a commitment form.

☐ **Leaders: trained and encouraged (Step 5-6-7)**
Your leaders need to know what to do and feel confident about doing it.

☐ **Identify those who may need to develop leadership skills**
Some of your leaders will be less skilled than others. Identify those who need help before your small groups begin. Your structure will grow stronger by helping leaders improve. Struggling leaders often don't last without this type of support.

☐ **Get curriculum to leaders (Step 4)**
Make your curriculum available a week or two before small groups begin. This should give them plenty of time to prepare and contact you with questions. Again, you'll value your leaders' time by giving them curriculum that is easy to teach and requires minimal preparation.

☐ **Get the word out (Step 8)**
Let students know when your small groups will be starting, why they'll want to sign up, and how they can sign up. Promotion should begin at least one month prior to launching your small group program.

☐ **See if the promotion is working**
Talk to several different students and ask if they are planning to commit to a small group. If they have no idea what you're talking about, then you'll need to step up your promotion efforts.

LAUNCH your program!

Now that you've finished reading through this step, take another look over this checklist and make a list that is specific to your church environment. It's getting close...keep going.

TIP   >   DON'T PANIC!

>> No matter how much preparation and leadership you pour into this HUGE task, you will still have problems. Plan to closely observe small groups for 3 or 4 weeks so you can troubleshoot big issues. As the lead youthworker, you might consider not leading a small group during the first year. This will free you up to fill-in for leaders who have emergencies or take a new group when one becomes too large. It will also make troubleshooting easier.   <<

STEP 10 > MAINTAIN, EVALUATE, AND LEAD

>> Continue training, evaluate everything, troubleshoot problems, make adjustments:

Meet regularly with your leadership team... and focus on encouragement
Provide short, on-going training tools for your leaders
Meet with key leaders and rookies regularly
Look for relational conflicts to smooth over
Evaluate the health of your small groups
Be easily accessible to your leaders for troubleshooting problems
Make wise adjustments

I'm the furthest thing from a mechanic, but even I know nothing continues to run on its own forever. At some point, everything needs maintenance. Your ministry is no exception. Like a car, it needs frequent re-fueling, consistent tune-ups, and occasionally (unfortunately) major overhauls. Without diligent leadership, more overhauls are necessary, and they usually cost big.

Once you get your small group ministry off the ground and running, it will still need your attention and leadership. Here are some ideas to help you maintain and grow your small group ministry.

Meet regularly with your leadership team... and focus on encouragement
Your small group leaders are going to be doing some tough work. As you know, spending time with students isn't the most affirming job in the world. Most leaders are busy; families, jobs, and responsibilities . . . and busy people don't often feel encouraged. Because of this and the need to get them more training, your regular gatherings (or volunteer staff meetings) will become a great time for you to breathe life into tired leaders. When I meet with my leadership team I want to make sure they...

- Know they are loved.
- Know they are not in this alone.
- Know they are not the only ones struggling.
- Receive some practical training.
- Get some basic announcements about the direction of the ministry.

During your monthly meetings, it is important for you to spend time training them. Surround your training with some food, a little fun, and a lot of encouragement.

When I hear of leaders doing something special with their small groups, I'll recognize them at the training meeting. It means a lot to small group leaders when they get noticed for something they're doing with their students. Plus, it sets a good example for the other leaders that youth ministry is being done, there's more happening than they can keep track of, and other leaders are doing things to minister to students.

Provide short, on-going training tools for your leaders
In Step 5, you created a specific job description for your leadership team. Your expectations can become the "backbone" of your leadership training. In addition to this, throughout the year, increase their skills by giving them short, practical training tools.

Meet with key leaders and rookies regularly
Since this ministry can quickly grow beyond you, you'll need to gather input from others to see how the leaders are doing and how the groups are going. Spending extra time with your "superstar" leaders will be a great way to see if the vision and values for your small group ministry are being fulfilled. You'll also want to give them a little extra encouragement since they are probably the ones running the ministry for you!

TIP > **PROVIDE BABYSITTING**

>> You can value and support your leaders by having some of your students offer free babysitting for those adults who would have to pay to attend training. You don't want your training meetings to cost your leaders money or cause extra financial stress on their family. Free babysitting is a simple way you can show thoughtfulness and appreciation. <<

Also, keep your rookie leaders on your radar. They will need more attention to help them be effective small group leaders since they are more likely to be discouraged and make mistakes. Be available to help them learn how to be leaders and discover how God has gifted them.

Look for relational conflicts to smooth over

If a relational conflict happens in your ministry (between a leader and a student, or two students, or with a parent) you will want to know about it. By being aware, you'll be able to take steps to do "damage control" and bring insight to the situation.

Nobody likes conflict, and the few people who do like it usually aren't good at reconciling it. Most people avoid conflict at all costs, and once it comes, they try their best to forget it. Since these are true, you'll need to look for it. Occasionally, directly ask your leaders if they have been involved with any relational conflict related to small groups. This way, you'll be able to put out small fires rather than being blindsided by roaring firestorms of conflict.

Evaluate the health of your small groups

There is no one way to evaluate the effectiveness of a small group program. Since no one knows it better than you, you ought to determine a simple yet effective method for evaluating this part of your ministry. You don't need to come up with something elaborate; keep it simple. But make sure it's not so simple that it isn't helpful. Here are a few areas to evaluate:

Attendance: How many students are in groups?

Most of us in youth ministry either put too much emphasis on numbers, or not enough. Numbers aren't everything, but they are important. If your small groups are smaller after a few months, then something might be wrong. I've found that when students are cared for, they typically grow. When they grow, they bring their friends... and the groups will grow.

Turnover: Are your students consistent?

If many of your students are inconsistent and flaky with their commitment to small group, then something might need to change.

Backdoor: Are you keeping most of your visitors?

If you have a small "backdoor," your small groups are enjoying a level of success as visitors are feeling comfortable enough to come back and get connected.

Buzzworthy: What's the word about your small groups?

If positive things are happening with your small groups, then students, parents, leaders, and host homes are going to be talking highly about your ministry. Be looking for what most people say, because there will be some critics who can always find something to complain about. Since you've designed this ministry for your students, frequently seek impromptu and informal one-on-one meetings. Ask them about their small group experience and probe beyond surface answers.

Be easily accessible to your leaders for troubleshooting problems

This probably goes without saying, but make sure your leaders can reach you when they need help (within reason: you don't need to be passing out curriculum in the middle of your anniversary dinner).

Make wise adjustments

As a leader, you'll need to make changes. This difficult topic has given birth to thousands of leadership books. Remember to keep in prayer as you consider what changes ought to be made. Don't shy away from something just because it's difficult; instead, move slowly and lay the groundwork before you "pull the trigger."

>> **Last words**

We're under no illusion that since you have read all these steps, we've equipped you to be the grand master of small group structure. Hopefully, you've learned a lot and you'll continue on the journey of growing and learning (as we are). It's our prayer that you'll feel encouraged because you read some actions that can help make small groups a reality in your ministry. We wanted this notebook to minimize some problems by maximizing some step-by-step actions.

Again, there is no one way to do everything relating to small groups, but you probably can't go wrong if you follow these steps in a logical manner.

Please send us your thoughts, comments, questions, and ideas as they relate to small groups. We can't guarantee that we'll answer every question, but we will be able to consider what you write during our next version/re-write of this resource. Your input could help others.

Thanks for taking the time to learn, lead, and love,

Doug Fields and Matt McGill
www.simplyyouthministry.com

CROSS REFERENCE > **STEP 10: MAINTAIN, EVALUATE, AND LEAD**

>> If you want to read more information that might help you with this step, you can check out the pages in Purpose Driven Youth Ministry (PDYM). Also, resources in Part 2 of this notebook that correspond with this step have resource titles listed below.

Meet regularly with your leadership team... and focus on encouragement
PDYM 302-304

>> **Related resources in Part 2:**

Meet regularly with your leadership team... and focus on encouragement
Letter to Coaches 129
Letter to Small Group Leaders 130
Letter to Division Leaders 131
Letter to Host Homes 132
Thank You Letter to Small Group Leaders 138

Provide short, on-going training tools for your leaders
Host Homes and Family Friendly Ministry 147
Four Keys For Leading Your Small Group 148
Milestones of Understanding 149
Prayer Request Sheet 150
Small Group Phone Book 151
Some Basic Small Group Dos and Don'ts 152
How to Listen Well 154
The Art of Asking Questions 155
Teaching Different Kinds of Truth 160
Small Group Leader Orientation Booklet 161
Small Group Coach Orientation Booklet 174
Small Group Division Leader Orientation Booklet 178
Small Group Quick Reference Card 180
Small Group Division Leader Meeting Agenda 181
Coach/Division Leader Tasks/Questions 182
Small Group Leader Application and References 183
Small Group Leader Evaluation 190
Ministry Resource List 191

SMALL GROUPS
From Start to Finish >>

PART TWO > Practical Tools and Resources

SMALL GROUPS
From Start to Finish >>

RESOURCES > Contents

> **THE FORGIVENESS OF JESUS**

>> **How to Use this Curriculum**

Basic Schedule

6:40	leaders meet for quick prayer
7:00-7:15	students arrive/hang out (greet visitors!!)
7:15-7:25	introduce the lesson
7:25-7:40	teaching groups "study"
7:40-8:10	teaching groups "teach" the other groups
8:10-8:50	small group time
8:50-9:00	hang out...boot students out of the house

Curriculum Overview

Lesson Objectives/Overview
This section is to help orient you to the purpose of each lesson. Your job is to help instill these truths into your students IN ANY WAY YOU WANT...if you want be creative and do something different, great!

Large Group Time
Once you officially get your Bible Study started, introduce the topic to your entire group, and then break them into "teaching groups." Each teaching group is assigned a passage for study, when they are finished they will teach the rest of your Bible study (detailed instructions are included with each lesson).

Small Group Time
A small group is one adult leader and 3 to 10 students (some groups are bigger, and this is a problem—we need more leaders to split those groups). This is your time TO FORM MEANINGFUL RELATIONSHIPS with your students...make the most of this time, as it is VERY EASY to waste. You have three goals for this time:

- Bible study: digging deeper into God's truth
- Personal applications, encouragements, accountability
- Sharing and prayer requests

What's the Next Step?
As a spiritual mentor, you should think about where you think your students need to grow next...this doesn't mean you are controlling their life, you are simply responding to how the Spirit is leading you to make a difference in your students' lives.

Although you should be on the look out for specific areas for spiritual growth (e.g. Tommy is too selfish), you should also encourage personal spiritual growth (HABITS), serving in a ministry (ministry teams), and sharing the good news with unbelievers (friendship evangelism).

The Forgiveness of Jesus

These objectives are provided to help orient you to the purpose and goals for this lesson.

Lesson Objectives
Understanding (knowledge, facts, or insights your students ought to learn)

To know that Jesus has the authority to forgive our sins, and that his compassion is the antidote to our shame and guilt

Reflection (personal truths your students ought to think about on their own)

Honest consideration of our personal faults so that we might rest more in God's grace

Impact (life change: actions your students ought to adopt in obedience to God's Word)

To commit to asking God for forgiveness at least once every day next week

Lesson Overview

When Jesus came into the world and started forgiving sins, the religious leaders of his day were shocked and outraged...only God had the authority to forgive sins and remove the guilt from people. The miracles and signs Jesus performed confirmed both that he was God and that he had authority to forgive, but the leaders were blind to this truth.

Forgiveness is not a one way street. God does not randomly select some people to receive automatic forgiveness. There's an element of responsibility upon the person being forgiven: they have to ask. Jesus' prayer for his murderers could not bring about their salvation and forgiveness without their change in heart, without faith or repentance.

When a person runs to God for forgiveness, amazing things happen: God forgets about our sin...I don't know how this happens, but it does.

As we relate to others, forgiveness is not an option for us as Christians. There is no limit to the number of times a Christian ought to forgive. There is no sin too intense, no consequence too devastating which allows a Christian to withhold forgiveness. We'll never have to forgive others more than God has forgiven us.

Large Group Time
Introduction (orient your Area Bible Study to the lesson)

Discussion Starter Questions

When it comes to relationships with others, why do you think forgiveness is so powerful?

Will someone share a story where you had to ask for forgiveness....how did this experience make an impact on you?

Even though we know how important forgiveness is, why do you think it's so hard for people in general to be forgiving?

Fill In Sentences
THE FORGIVENESS OF JESUS

No one in this world is perfect, and we all have to deal with shame and guilt for things we've done in the past.

Ultimately, there are only two options for dealing with our guilt: we can either hide and ignore it, or bring it to God, asking for his forgiveness. God knows our greatest needs, this is why he sent Jesus 2,000 years ago.

In this study, we'll take a look at two stories from Jesus' ministry that display HOW AND WHY Jesus was able to forgive sins, and WHAT this means for our lives.

My notes
(things I want to cover in the introduction)

Large Group Time (continued)
Bible Discussion (large group Bible study and discussion)

Break into Teaching Groups
This is the time for you to break your large group into FIVE different groups. Make them random and see to it that these groups change each week. Give the following instructions to your ABS:

We're going to break into 5 groups, and each group is going to study their assigned passage for 10 to 15 minutes. When they are done, everyone will come together and each group will do two things:

(a) explain/retell the passage in their own words (some groups like to use skits...but you don't have to!), and

(b) give a one sentence summary of the passage (for this week, the summary should answer the question: 'What is God's purpose for us?')

As you break into groups, don't send any adult leaders with the groups—LET YOUR STUDENTS DEAL WITH THE PASSAGE ON THEIR OWN. After a couple of minutes, the teacher/coach should walk around to check on and help each group.

Teaching Group Bible Passages

Group 1
Mark 2:1-5

1 A few days later, when Jesus again entered Capernaum, the people heard that he had come home. 2 So many gathered that there was no room left, not even outside the door, and he preached the word to them. 3 Some men came, bringing to him a paralytic, carried by four of them. 4 Since they could not get him to Jesus because of the crowd, they made an opening in the roof above Jesus and, after digging through it, lowered the mat the paralyzed man was lying on. 5 When Jesus saw their faith, he said to the paralytic, "Son, your sins are forgiven."

Group 2
Mark 2:6-12

6 Now some teachers of the law were sitting there, thinking to themselves, 7 "Why does this fellow talk like that? He's blaspheming! Who can forgive sins but God alone?" 8 Immediately Jesus knew in his spirit that this was what they were thinking in their hearts, and he said to them, "Why are you thinking these things? 9 Which is easier: to say to the paralytic, `Your sins are forgiven,' or to say, `Get up, take your mat and walk'? 10 But that you may know that the Son of Man has authority on earth to forgive sins . . . ." He said to the paralytic, 11 "I tell you, get up, take your mat and go home." 12 He got up, took his mat and walked out in full view of them all. This amazed everyone and they praised God, saying, "We have never seen anything like this!"

Group 3
John 8:1-8

1 But Jesus went to the Mount of Olives. 2 At dawn he appeared again in the temple courts, where all the people gathered around him, and he sat down to teach them. 3 The teachers of the law and the Pharisees brought in a woman caught in adultery. They made her stand before the group 4 and said to Jesus, "Teacher, this woman was caught in the act of adultery. 5 In the Law, Moses commanded us to stone such women. Now what do you say?" 6 They were using this question as a trap, in order to have a basis for accusing him. But Jesus bent down and started to write on the ground with his finger. 7 When they kept on questioning him, he straightened up and said to them, "If any one of you is without sin, let him be the first to throw a stone at her." 8 Again he stooped down and wrote on the ground.

Group 4
John 8:9-11
9 At this, those who heard began to go away one at a time, the older ones first, until only Jesus was left, with the woman still standing there. 10 Jesus straightened up and asked her, "Woman, where are they? Has no one condemned you?" 11 "No one, sir," she said. "Then neither do I condemn you," Jesus declared. "Go now and leave your life of sin."

Large Group Time (continued)
Wrap Up (tie up loose ends and drive home the key lessons)

As you prepare for this lesson, make note of the TWO or THREE key truths you want to emphasize to your students. Also, be sure to clear up confusing things.

Walk through these once all of the TEACHING GROUPS have shared their findings.

Small Group Time
Bible Study and Discussion (talking about God's Word and making personal applications)
Mark 2:1-12
1 A few days later, when Jesus again entered Capernaum, the people heard that he had come home. 2 So many gathered that there was no room left, not even outside the door, and he preached the word to them. 3 Some men came, bringing to him a paralytic, carried by four of them. 4 Since they could not get him to Jesus because of the crowd, they made an opening in the roof above Jesus and, after digging through it, lowered the mat the paralyzed man was lying on. 5 When Jesus saw their faith, he said to the paralytic, "Son, your sins are forgiven." 6 Now some teachers of the law were sitting there, thinking to themselves, 7 "Why does this fellow talk like that? He's blaspheming! Who can forgive sins but God alone?" 8 Immediately Jesus knew in his spirit that this was what they were thinking in their hearts, and he said to them, "Why are you thinking these things? 9 Which is easier: to say to the paralytic, `Your sins are forgiven,' or to say, `Get up, take your mat and walk'? 10 But that you may know that the Son of Man has authority on earth to forgive sins . . . ." He said to the paralytic, 11 "I tell you, get up, take your mat and go home." 12 He got up, took his

mat and walked out in full view of them all. This amazed everyone and they praised God, saying, "We have never seen anything like this!"

Discussion Questions
- After reading this passage, does anyone have any questions?
- What doesn't make sense?
- What seems strange or weird?
- Why do you think the house where Jesus was teaching was so full?
- Why did Jesus forgive the sins of the paralytic?
- How did the teachers of the law respond?
- What does blaspheming mean?
- Why did the teachers of the law think that Jesus was blaspheming?
- Which is more amazing, forgiving sins or healing a person?
- What does this story teach us about being a good friend?
- Would you say your life is like the friends who brought the paralytic to Jesus?
- Are you bringing your friends to Christ? Or would you say you're more like a Pharisee, judging others harshly?
- What significance does forgiveness have in your life?
- Why is forgiveness so powerful?
- How does this story affect you day to day?
- Share one specific way that it could affect you in the week to come.

Encouraging Your Small Group To Take the Next Step
Every night this week, make a commitment to ask God for forgiveness for the things you've done wrong...try to be as specific as possible, and ask him to help you be better at resting in his grace.

Small Group Time (continued)
Sharing and Prayer (sharing and prayer and holding one another accountable)

Prayer Request Super Sheet

Name:
Request:
Date:
Follow Up/Answer:

Name:
Request:
Date:
Follow Up/Answer:

Name:
Request:
Date:
Follow Up/Answer:

Name:
Request:
Date:
Follow Up/Answer:

Name:
Request:
Date:
Follow Up/Answer:

Name:
Request:
Date:
Follow Up/Answer:

Name:
Request:
Date:
Follow Up/Answer:

Name:
Request:
Date:
Follow Up/Answer:

> THE FORGIVENESS OF JESUS

>> Introduction

No one in this world is perfect; we all have to deal with shame and guilt for things we've done in the past.

Ultimately, there are only two options for dealing with our guilt: we can (a) either hide and ignore it, or (b) bring it to God, asking for his forgiveness. God knows our greatest need, this is why he sent Jesus 2000 years ago.

In this study, we'll take a look at two stories from Jesus' ministry that display HOW AND WHY Jesus was able to forgive sins, and WHAT this means for our lives.

Teaching Groups (1 & 2)

Teaching Group instructions
We're going to break into 5 groups, and each group is going to study their assigned passage for 10 to 15 minutes. When they are done, everyone will come together and each group will do two things:

Explain/retell the passage in their own words (some groups like to use skits...but you don't have to!) and give a one sentence summary of the passage as it relates to tonight's theme.

Group 1: Mark 2:1-5 – one sentence summary
1 A few days later, when Jesus again entered Capernaum, the people heard that he had come home. 2 So many gathered that there was no room left, not even outside the door, and he preached the word to them. 3 Some men came, bringing to him a paralytic, carried by four of them. 4 Since they could not get him to Jesus because of the crowd, they made an opening in the roof above Jesus and, after digging through it, lowered the mat the paralyzed man was lying on. 5 When Jesus saw their faith, he said to the paralytic, "Son, your sins are forgiven."

Group 2: Mark 2:6-12 – one sentence summary

6 Now some teachers of the law were sitting there, thinking to themselves, 7 "Why does this fellow talk like that? He's blaspheming! Who can forgive sins but God alone?" 8 Immediately Jesus knew in his spirit that this was what they were thinking in their hearts, and he said to them, "Why are you thinking these things? 9 Which is easier: to say to the paralytic, 'Your sins are forgiven,' or to say, 'Get up, take your mat and walk'? 10 But that you may know that the Son of Man has authority on earth to forgive sins . . . ." He said to the paralytic, 11 "I tell you, get up, take your mat and go home." 12 He got up, took his mat and walked out in full view of them all. This amazed everyone and they praised God, saying, "We have never seen anything like this!"

Teaching Groups (3 & 4)

Group 3: John 8:1-8 – one sentence summary

1 But Jesus went to the Mount of Olives. 2 At dawn he appeared again in the temple courts, where all the people gathered around him, and he sat down to teach them. 3 The teachers of the law and the Pharisees brought in a woman caught in adultery. They made her stand before the group 4 and said to Jesus, "Teacher, this woman was caught in the act of adultery. 5 In the Law, Moses commanded us to stone such women. Now what do you say?" 6 They were using this question as a trap, in order to have a basis for accusing him. But Jesus bent down and started to write on the ground with his finger. 7 When they kept on questioning him, he straightened up and said to them, "If any one of you is without sin, let him be the first to throw a stone at her." 8 Again he stooped down and wrote on the ground.

Group 4: John 8:9-11 – one sentence summary

9 At this, those who heard began to go away one at a time, the older ones first, until only Jesus was left, with the woman still standing there. 10 Jesus straightened up and asked her, "Woman, where are they? Has no one condemned you?" 11 "No one, sir," she said. "Then neither do I condemn you," Jesus declared. "Go now and leave your life of sin."

Small Group

Mark 2:1-12 – notes and such

1 A few days later, when Jesus again entered Capernaum, the people heard that he had come home. 2 So many gathered that there was no room left, not even outside the door, and he preached the word to them. 3 Some men came, bringing to him a paralytic, carried by four of them. 4 Since they could not get him to Jesus because of the crowd, they made an opening in the roof above Jesus and, after digging through it, lowered the mat the paralyzed man was lying on. 5 When Jesus saw their faith, he said to the paralytic, "Son, your sins are forgiven." 6 Now some teachers of the law were sitting there, thinking to themselves, 7 "Why does this fellow talk like that? He's blaspheming! Who can forgive sins but God alone?" 8 Immediately Jesus knew in his spirit that this was what they were thinking in their hearts, and he said to them, "Why are you thinking these things? 9 Which is easier: to say to the paralytic, `Your sins are forgiven,' or to say, `Get up, take your mat and walk'? 10 But that you may know that the Son of Man has authority on earth to forgive sins . . . ." He said to the paralytic, 11 "I tell you, get up, take your mat and go home." 12 He got up, took his mat and walked out in full view of them all. This amazed everyone and they praised God, saying, "We have never seen anything like this!"

The Next Step

Every night this week, make a commitment to ask God for forgiveness for the things you've done wrong...try to be as specific as possible, and ask him to help you be better at resting in his grace.

> **THE LIFE OF JESUS**

WEEK 1 >> **The Incarnation**
John 1:1-8
John 1:19-14
John 1:15-18
Philippians 2:5-11 - Attitude of Jesus
John 1:1-18 - The WORD became Flesh

WEEK 2 >> **The Life and Teachings of John the Baptist**
Luke 3:1-9
Luke 3:10-20 - The Voice Calling in the Desert
Matthew 11:1-6
Matthew 11:7-15
Matthew 11:1-15 - John's Question from Prison

WEEK 3 >> **The Baptism and Temptation of Jesus**
Matthew 3:13-17
Matthew 4:1-4
Matthew 4:5-11
Hebrews 4:14-16 - A Great High Priest
Matthew 4:1-11 - Temptation in the Desert

WEEK 4 >> **Ministry Begins**
Luke 4:14-21
Luke 4:22-30
Luke 4:31-37 - A Popular Savior
John 2:1-12 - A Wedding in Need of a Miracle
Luke 4:14-30 - Today Scripture Is Fulfilled in Your Hearing

WEEK 5 >> **Jesus' Model of Discipleship**
Luke 9:18-27 - Who Do You Say that I Am?
Luke 9:57-62 - No Place to Put My Head, No Time to Look Back
Luke 14:28-33
John 21:15-17 - Do You Love Me?
Luke 14:28-33 - Counting the Cost

WEEK 6 >> **The Opposition: Pharisees, Sadducees, and Teachers of the Law**
Mark 7:1-13
Mark7 :14-23 - The Heart of Cleanliness
John 8:1-11 - Forgiven Adulteress SWITCH TO LUKE 7:1-10
Matthew 23:25-28 - Clean the Inside of the Cup
Matthew 21:23-27 - By What Authority?

WEEK 7 >> **I AM**
John 6:35-40 - Bread of Life
John 8:12-18 - Light of the World
John 10:11-16 - Good Shepherd
John 14:6-14
John 6:35-51 - Way, Truth, and the Life

WEEK 8 >> **Jesus the Healer**
John 9:1-12 - Blind Man Healed for the Glory of God
John 11:38-44 - Dead Man Healed for the Glory of God
Mark 3:1-6 - Hand Healed on the Sabbath
Matthew 15:21-28 - Gentile Woman Healed Because of Her Faith
John 9:1-12

WEEK 9 >> **Jesus the Forgiver of Sin**
Mark 2:1-5
Mark 2:6-12
John 8:1-8
John 8:9-11 - Forgiven Adulteress
Mark 2:1-12 - Paralytic and his Four Friends

WEEK 10 >> **Peter's Ups and Downs**
Matthew 14:25-31 - Water Walk
Matthew 16:13-19 - "Who Do You Say that I am?"
Matthew 26:69-75 - Peter's Denial
John 21:15-19 - Peter Reinstated
Matthew 14:25-31

WEEK 11 >> **Who Did Jesus Hang Out With?**
John 3:1-7 - Nicodemus
John 4:7-15 - Woman at the Well
Luke 19:1-9 - Zacchaeus
Luke 17:11-19 - 10 Lepers healed
John 4:7-15

WEEK 12 >> **The Few. The Chosen. The Apostles**
Matthew 4:21-22; Mark 9:38-40 - John
Luke 8:51-56 - Peter, James, and John
John 20:24-29 - Thomas
Matthew 27:1-10 - Judas
Acts 2:42-47 - the Disciples and the Early Church

WEEK 13 >> **The Final Night of Jesus**
John 13:1, 4-8, 12-15 - Passover Supper
Matthew 26:20-30 - Prediction of Judas' Betrayal
Matthew 26:31-35 - Jesus Predicts Peter's Denial
Matthew 26:36-46 - Jesus Prays in a Garden
John 13:1, 4-8, 12-15 - Passover Supper

WEEK 14 >> **The Crucifixion of Jesus**
Matthew 27:11-26
Matthew 27:27-31
Matthew 27:32-44
Matthew 27:45-56
John 19:16-27

WEEK 15 >> **The Resurrection of Jesus**
Matthew 28:1-10 - Resurrection
Matthew 28:11-15 - Deceit of the Priests
John 20:19-23 - Appearances
Luke 24:13-27
Luke 24:13-27

> ## THE TEACHINGS OF JESUS

WEEK 1 >> **Stories That Will Change Your Life**
Luke 14:16-24	The Great Banquet
Matthew 7:24-27	The Wise and Foolish
Matthew 25:14-30	The Talents
Matthew 20:1-16	The Workers
Matthew 20:1-16	

WEEK 2 >> **To Save the Lost...**
Matthew 13:44-46	Treasures and Pearls
Luke 15:4-10 One	Lost Sheep
Matthew 9:16-17	Patches and Wineskins
Matthew 13:31-33	The Mustard Seed
Luke 15:11-32	The Lost Son

WEEK 3 >> **Faith Like a Child**
Luke 16:19-31	Rich Man and Lazarus
Luke 18:9-14	Two Kinds of Prayers
Luke 13:6-9	Unfruitful Fig Tree
Matthew 18:1-9	Like a Child

WEEK 4 >> **The Kingdom of God**
John 3:1-18	Jesus and Nicodemus
Luke 14:28-32	Counting the Cost
Matthew 13:24-30	Wheat and Weeds
Matthew 21:28-32	Two Sons

WEEK 5 >> **The Good Shepherd**
John 10:10-19	The Good Shepherd
Matthew 18:23-34	The Selfish Servant
Luke 20:9-16	The Evil Farmers and the Vineyard
Luke 12:16-20	The Rich Fool
Matthew 25:1-12	Ten Bridesmaids
John 10:1-19	

WEEK 6 >> **The Light Of the World**
John 3:19-21	
Luke 11:33-37	
1 John 1:5-7; 2:9-10	
2 Corinthians 4:4-6	

WEEK 7 >> **The Sermon on the Mount, Part 1**
Matthew 5:1-3, 7
Matthew 5:1-2,4,8
Matthew5:1-2,5,9
Matthew 5:1-2,6,10
Matthew 5:11-16

WEEK 8 >> **The Sermon on the Mount, Part 2**
Matthew 5:21-24
Matthew 5:27-30
Matthew 5:33-37
Matthew 5:38-42
Matthew 5:43-48

WEEK 9 >> **The Sermon on the Mount, Part 3**
Matthew 6:1-4
Matthew 6:5-8
Matthew 6:9-15
Matthew 6:16-18
Matthew 6:19-24

WEEK 10 >> **The Sermon on the Mount, Part 4**
Matthew 6:25-27
Matthew 7:1-5
Matthew 7:15-20
Matthew 7:24-27
Matthew 6:25-34

CURRICULUM > Curriculum Survey

> CURRICULUM SURVEY

>> Respond to each question by circling the appropriate number.

A. The curriculum has been a helpful tool to facilitate my small group.

1	2	3	4	5
Agree				Disagree!

B. My favorite part of the curriculum is editing typos.

1	2	3	4	5
Agree				Disagree!

C. The curriculum is easy to follow and prepare for.

1	2	3	4	5
Agree				Disagree!

This would make it easier to prep:

D. I like the 'Pause & Reflect' section.

1	2	3	4	5
Agree				Disagree!

E. Some of the biblical passages are too difficult and I need help with their meaning.

1	2	3	4	5
Agree				Disagree!

F. Concerning the small group time

Introduction (fill-ins, 10 minutes)

1	2	3	4	5
Really love				Really don't love

Teaching Groups Study

1	2	3	4	5
Really love				Really don't love

Teaching Groups Teach

1	2	3	4	5
Really love				Really don't love

"What's the Point" fill-ins

1	2	3	4	5
Really love				Really don't love

Small Group Time

1	2	3	4	5
Really love				Really don't love

Bible Study & Discussion

1	2	3	4	5
Really love				Really don't love

Application Fill-ins

1	2	3	4	5
Really love				Really don't love

Sharing and Prayer Requests

1	2	3	4	5
Really love				Really don't love

G. As a teacher I need to grow in this area:

H. As a small group leader, I need to grow in this way:

I. How long does it take you to prepare for ONE small group lesson?
_____ minutes _____hours _____days _____weeks

J. Do you make your prep time separate from your quiet time?
Can your preparation time for small group also serve as your quiet time?

K. Here are some thoughts, changes, or comments I'd like to make:

> SMALL GROUP EVALUATION GUIDE

>> Spend at least 10 minutes examining how well your small group went. There are different sections for the teacher, small group leader, and coach. Work through the section(s) that apply to your role. Being intentional to discern the effectiveness of your ministry will yield insights, improve your ministry, and increase your influence with the students God has entrusted to your care.

Small Group Leader Examination Questions:

1. I was an effective small group leader this week.

1	2	3	4	5
Agree				Disagree

Write down goals or action steps if needed.

2. As a small group, we spent enough time talking about the Bible passage assigned for small group discussion and made personal applications.

1	2	3	4	5
Agree				Disagree

3. Most of my students felt spiritually challenged this week.

1	2	3	4	5
Agree				Disagree

4. I kept my small group reasonably focused.

1	2	3	4	5
Agree				Disagree

5. Everyone in my small group had an opportunity to participate in the discussion.

1	2	3	4	5
Agree				Disagree

6. I have a good gauge of my students' spiritual condition and have some ideas for encouraging them to continue to grow.

1	2	3	4	5
Agree				Disagree

7. I feel like I KNOW the students God has entrusted to my care (family issues, major struggles, how they like to spend their free time, etc.)

1	2	3	4	5
Agree				Disagree

>> **Teacher Examination Questions:**

[At Saddleback Church, small groups meet in one home. Within every home, we have a designated teacher. The teacher will teach in the living room and then all the small groups will meet throughout the house. The teacher is also a small group leader.]

1. Did you start the teaching on time (7:15-7:20)?   Yes   No
Write down goals or action steps if needed.

2. How did the introduction to the lesson go?
1   2   3   4   5
Poor   Great

3. The students had some good discussion during the teaching times.
1   2   3   4   5
Disagree   Agree

4. The curriculum helps you explain each passage.
1   2   3   4   5
Disagree   Agree

5. Everyone walked away from the large group teaching time into small groups with a basic understanding of each passage.
1   2   3   4   5
Disagree   Agree

6. Did you break for small groups on time (7:45-8:00)?   Yes   No
If not, what could you do next week to make this happen?

>> **Coach Examination Questions**

(At Saddleback, each home group has a veteran leader whom we call the coach. This leader oversees all the small groups and everything that happens within the house. The coach may or may not be the teacher.)

1. All of my small group leaders showed up on time (6:45). Yes No Write down goals or action steps if needed.

2. The vision and values of small groups were carried out this week.

1	2	3	4	5
Disagree				Agree

3. How many visitors showed up this week?   1   2   3   4   5 _____

4. Is a leader going to follow up on each visitor?   Yes   No

5. Did you take attendance for this week?   Yes   No

6. Is a leader going to follow up on the absent students? Yes   No

> CONSIDERATIONS WHEN WRITING CURRICULUM

>> 1. Determine the potential audience and the biblical purpose for the program where the curriculum will be used. What kind of students will be at your program? (believer, seeker, leader, stumbler, etc...) What biblical purpose do you want to fulfill?

Fellowship Curriculum
Perhaps: creative interaction, easier passages, lots of interaction

Discipleship Curriculum
Perhaps: verse-by-verse, lots of questions and discussion, homework assignments

Ministry Curriculum
Perhaps: centered around work projects, reflective type questions ("How did you feel building the house?" "Why is serving important?")

Worship Curriculum
Perhaps: deep, introspective questions which center around an individual's personal experiences with God and their personal world view

Evangelism Curriculum
Perhaps: answers questions non-believers would ask, an "apologetic" flavor

2. Look at other people's material. Table of Contents: for major themes and concepts. Lessons: structure ideas, and rework questions.

3. Create a simple structure that works, and be open to making changes if needed.

4. Write general questions, especially if other leaders will be teaching your curriculum.

5. Provide something for your students to take home.

Students need to have balanced opportunities to talk about:
       specific biblical passages
       theological truths
       personal life issues
       personal applications of truth

Typical Ways of Relating to God's Truth

• Learn truth passively.
> God's Word is heard, with little or "no" change.

• Discuss truth personally.
> God's Word is talked about, questions are asked, interaction between God's people.

• Discover truth passionately.
> God's Word becomes personal and real, life change is inevitable.

• Discern truth in life situations.
> God's Word is gleaned from personal experience and is applied with wisdom.

• Teach truth to others.
> The highest privilege and duty of all believers; here God's Word is communicated.

> FIRST NIGHT OF SMALL GROUPS

>> Here is the schedule for the first night of Area Bible Study Small Groups. Prior to arriving, touch base with your small group leaders and see if they can bring snacks (or make calls to key students and/or parents). This will give the first 15-20 minutes a fun, relational feel.

7-7:20pm
Spend the first 20 minutes greeting and doing relational ministry. Work to introduce "new" (in a sense, they are all new, but this refers to the person who has never been to an Area Bible Study Small Group before) students to other students—make sure your leaders are trying to meet students and remember names.

7:20-7:40pm
Name Game—go around a circle: Give 2 bucks to whoever can remember EVERYONE's name. You may want to add this element—have each student say his/her name and favorite food that starts with the first letter of his/her first name. It may be easier to remember names this way.

7:40-7:45pm
Spend a few minutes casting vision to the students about your excitement for what Area Bible Study Small Groups can be this year. You will want to include the following...

• the students will get out of a small group what they put in;
• "I'm committed to this, all our leaders are committed, you be committed and watch incredible things happen,"
• that Area Bible Study Small Group is comprised of two kinds of nights...
    - type one: in the home, teaching time, and small group
    - type two: ABS.com (every 6-8 weeks) at the church property--communion, praise and worship;
• that the reason you are there is because you love God and you love to see what happens when students allow God to get a hold of their lives.

7:45-7:50pm
Break up into small groups. These same sex groups should be done ahead of time or you'll have mass chaos.

7:50-8:05pm
Do the student profile in small groups—we will try to provide pens or pencils for this to happen. Tell the students to answer as honestly as they can.

8:05-8:45pm
Go over student profiles to get to know your students. Have dialogue about the different questions. Instead of focusing on one student and having them give all of the answers, focus on each question, and have the students share their answers. This is less threatening, and it allows you to explore the answers in a group setting. Plus, it opens things up for more dialogue between the students. Make sure that you grab these profiles and get them to your coach at the end of the night!

8:45-8:55
Pray for the Area Bible Study Small Group year. You may want to ask for prayer requests (especially if you find that you have more than 10 minutes). Close the night in prayer, and make sure students help clean the host home.

8:55-9:05pm
Everybody leaves!

> SIX WAYS TO BE A STUDENT LEADER AT SMALL GROUPS

>> Small groups are a great place for student leaders to connect with other students on a level that is not normally possible at weekend services. Use this time to your advantage. Here are some ideas on how to be a leader at Area Bible Study Small Groups:

1. It is each student leader's responsibility to be a greeter within the home. Be friendly and introduce yourself to everyone, and be everyone's "friend". Socialize with your own friends, but make efforts to be a friendly face to unconnected people. Look for students who feel uncomfortable.

2. Remember people have been kind enough to give up their homes. As student leaders, set an example. Student leaders should try to arrive a little early to help set up and stay late to make sure everything looks better than when we arrived.

3. Each student leader should commit to pray weekly for their small groups and all the groups that meet within the home. Also, pray for adult leaders and thank God for the ministry they do.

4. Each student leader should also consider themselves an apprentice within their small group. Watch other leaders and see how they interact with students and lead small groups. You can grow as a leader by watching other leaders.

5. Outside of small groups, student leaders should be in a constant search for new students to join a small group. Because small groups are designed for Christians, you should be thinking of people who are interested in "Christian" things. This doesn't mean you can't or shouldn't invite non-believers, it's just not necessarily the best place for them to "check out church." On the other hand, most of the disruptions that happen in small groups come from students who aren't there to grow, connect, etc.

6. As a leader, you should be plugged into a small group for your benefit. Always feel open to share. Remember, leaders should be transparent. Don't let your duties as a student leader get in the way of your growth at a small group. Your spiritual growth is important!

> SOME BASIC ACCOUNTABILITY QUESTIONS

>> Weekly accountability is tough! Each time we meet, everyone will read all of the questions, take a few moments to examine their life, and share a response to at least one of the questions.

The Wonder Question
1. Have you maintained an attitude of awe and wonder toward God?
. . . or have you minimized him, placed him in a box, failing to contemplate his greatness?
Key issue: awe, wonderment, and WORSHIP versus ordinary, usual, and IDOLATRY.

The Priority Question
2. Have you maintained a personal (quiet) time with God?
. . . or have you allowed yourself to become too busy for God? Have you exchanged a vibrant, tender relationship filled with rich communication for a superficial acquaintance with God?
Key issue: time with God versus time without God.

The Morality Question
3. Have you maintained integrity with the way you live out your faith?
. . . or have you compromised what you know to be true with your actions?
Key issue: integrity versus compromise.

The Listening Question
4. Have you maintained a soft heart, sensitive to the things of God?
. . . or have you chosen to remain on the easy path, refusing to be challenged to move out of your comfort zone?
Key issue: uncomfortable versus comfortable

The Relationships Question
5. Have you maintained peaceful relationships and resolved conflicts to the best of your ability?
. . . or have you caused conflict or offense?
Key issue: peace versus conflict; resolved versus ignored.

Here are things I need to pray for this week:

> **WHAT WE CAN LEARN FROM GOD'S WORD**

>> When I read the Bible, I can look for:

I. Truth about God's character
God gave us the Bible so we could learn more about who he is. We don't need someone else to tell us EVERYTHING about God; we can learn on our own! Discover God on his own terms; he gave us the Bible so we could learn more about his character through alone time with him and his Word.

II. Truth about the way things are
God hasn't left us here on earth alone to figure things out on our own. Life can be difficult, but when we know "how the world works" we can make better, wiser decisions.

III. Truth about the way things were
God gave us the history in the Bible to teach us. The Bible isn't a history full of perfect people; instead, it details the lives of imperfect people like you and me. Their lives—good choices and bad—serve as an example to move us on to greater maturity. (See Hebrews 11:1-12:1)

IV. Truth about how we ought to act
The Bible doesn't only tell us about how things are or how they were; it also reveals a picture of how things ought to be. God's love for us is so great that he accepts us where we are; and his love is greater still because he doesn't want to leave us there. God gives us commands to follow for our benefit and well being.

When you read, here are four questions you can ask to help learn from the Bible:
1. What does this passage teach me about who God is, how he acts, what he likes?
2. What does this passage teach about the nature of the world (about the way things are)?
3. Does this passage have an example from the past that I can learn from?
4. What commands does this passage contain for me to follow with my life?

Some practical steps for becoming better at studying the Bible:
• Learn to view Bible study as a non-negotiable time throughout your week.
• Set aside a consistent time when you are at your best.
• Avoid the extremes of being ritualistic (mechanical) or slothful (lazy).
• Begin with some realistic goals and boundaries for your study time.
• Be open to God's Spirit.
• Fall in love with God like he's your best friend.

> SMALL GROUPS VISITOR'S GUIDE

>> Getting the most out of your small group time.

Welcome to our home! I've put together a few things to help you make the most out of your time each week. Thanks for coming; it's my prayer that you'll be challenged and encouraged in your faith and life.

Understanding why we have small groups

We meet to study the Bible.
"All Scripture is inspired by God and is useful to teach us what is true and to make us realize what is wrong in our lives. It straightens us out and teaches us to do what is right." 2 Tim. 3:16

We meet to grow closer to God.
God loves you more than you can imagine. He wants good things for your life, better things than you could ever dream! He wants you to learn more about him... so come ready to grow!

We meet because God changes lives.
Learning truth about God without allowing that truth to RADICALLY impact your life is a crime against God. He wants to make a difference IN your life and THROUGH your life. Make the decision to impact your world for Christ. You can do it! Live in obedience to what you know is right.

Things you can do to get the most from your small group

Commit to consistency and show up on time.
Be on time and show up at 7:00. If you have a schedule conflict, coming late is fine, but try to get here as close to 7:00 as possible.

Bring your Bible.
Bring your Bible so you can learn to use it, make notes in it, underline key verses, etc.

Develop a personal quiet time.
One of the great truths about your relationship with God is that you don't HAVE TO go to a church program in order to spend time with him and grow closer to him. In fact, if the only time you stop to focus on God is when you are "at church," then you're really missing out. Begin to develop your personal alone times with God, as this will push you into deeper spiritual maturity.

Stay mentally focused.
Since most of the time we'll be talking about God and important spiritual matters, do your best to remain focused. Everyone should be mentally involved and participate in the discussions. Not everyone feels like talking in front of others; THIS IS FINE, but you can still stay focused and learn.

Respect your small group.
Maintain confidentiality. Be honest with your questions, fears, struggles, etc. Refuse to "play it safe" and take a risk. Superficial relationships permeate EVERY aspect of our lives; don't let that sickness exist in your small group. Don't talk to make conversation, but share to make a difference.

> SPIRITUAL HEALTH ASSESSMENT

>> Spend some time answering the following questions. This isn't a test, it's a tool designed to help you evaluate where you are in your faith journey. When you are done, celebrate the areas where you consider yourself healthy, and think about how you can use those strengths to help others grow. Also, take some time to identify some potential growth areas. If you need help determining the next step you might take with your faith, sit down with your small group leader and talk about some ideas.

One last thought... take your time, go slowly, and be thorough.

Reach: The biblical purpose of Evangelism

I have committed to the Friendship Evangelism Challenge.
(strongly disagree)   1   2   3   4   5   (strongly agree)

I have been praying for my non-Christian friends.
(strongly disagree)   1   2   3   4   5   (strongly agree)

I have been inviting my non-Christian friends to the weekend services.
(strongly disagree)   1   2   3   4   5   (strongly agree)

I have been sharing my faith with others.
(strongly disagree)   1   2   3   4   5   (strongly agree)

I have been praying for opportunities to share about what Jesus has done in my life.
(strongly disagree)   1   2   3   4   5   (strongly agree)

People know I am a Christian by more than just my words alone. (Modeling Christ)
(strongly disagree)   1   2   3   4   5   (strongly agree)

I feel a strong compassion for the lost.
(strongly disagree)   1   2   3   4   5   (strongly agree)

I've taken class 401.
(strongly disagree)   1   2   3   4   5   (strongly agree)

SPIRITUAL HEALTH ASSESSMENT

Describe any significant conversations about God, church, etc. you've had with non-believers in the past month. Has your faith been challenged by any non-Christians? If yes, how?

What have been some difficulties you've faced with sharing your faith?

What have been some successes you've observed with your personal evangelism?

Connect: The biblical purpose of Fellowship

I meet consistently with a small group or a mentor.
(strongly disagree)   1   2   3   4   5   (strongly agree)

I feel connected with other Christians who hold me accountable.
(strongly disagree)   1   2   3   4   5   (strongly agree)

I feel I could talk with my small group leader if I needed help, advice, or support.
(strongly disagree)   1   2   3   4   5   (strongly agree)

My Christian friends are a significant source of strength and stability for my life.
(strongly disagree)   1   2   3   4   5   (strongly agree)

I regularly pray for my small group outside of the time we meet.
(strongly disagree)   1   2   3   4   5   (strongly agree)

I have resolved all major conflicts with other Christians...and non-Christians.
(strongly disagree)   1   2   3   4   5   (strongly agree)

I'm not bitter toward everyone I know.
(strongly disagree)   1   2   3   4   5   (strongly agree)

My family life has been great lately, especially with my immediate family.
(strongly disagree)   1   2   3   4   5   (strongly agree)

I feel like I've done all I possibly can to be a good son/daughter, and brother/sister.
(strongly disagree)   1   2   3   4   5   (strongly agree)

I am usually sensitive to the hurts/pains of others and respond in a caring way.
(strongly disagree)   1   2   3   4   5   (strongly agree)

I've taken class 101.
(strongly disagree)   1   2   3   4   5   (strongly agree)

List the five most significant relationships in your life right now and why these people are important to you.

What words would you use to describe the benefit you receive from being connected?

Has accountability been a serious part of your faith for the past month? Describe. Do you have an accountability partner? If so, what have you been doing to hold each other accountable?

What's something you feel you need to be held accountable for?

Grow: The biblical purpose of Discipleship

I have regular quiet times.
(strongly disagree)   1   2   3   4   5   (strongly agree)

I consistently grow in my quiet times with God.
(strongly disagree)   1   2   3   4   5   (strongly agree)

I don't need to increase the frequency of my quiet times.
(strongly disagree)   1   2   3   4   5   (strongly agree)

I feel like I'm closer to God this month that I did last month.
(strongly disagree)   1   2   3   4   5   (strongly agree)

I feel like I'm making better decisions this month when compared to last month.
(strongly disagree)   1   2   3   4   5   (strongly agree)

I meet consistently with an accountability partner for prayer and accountability.
(strongly disagree)   1   2   3   4   5   (strongly agree)

I regularly attend and grow as a result of attending church services.
(strongly disagree)   1   2   3   4   5   (strongly agree)

I consistently honor God with my finances by spending wisely.
(strongly disagree)   1   2   3   4   5   (strongly agree)

I consistently honor God with my finances by personal giving.
(strongly disagree)   1   2   3   4   5   (strongly agree)

I have been diligent with my school responsibilities (attendance, study, homework, not cheating).
(strongly disagree)   1   2   3   4   5   (strongly agree)

I regularly do in-depth Bible study on my own.
(strongly disagree)   1   2   3   4   5   (strongly agree)

I have taken class 201.
(strongly disagree)   1   2   3   4   5   (strongly agree)

Within the last month I've read the following from the Bible:

What are some things God has been teaching you lately?

What and when was the last verse you memorized? Describe the last time a memorized scripture helped you.

Discover: The biblical purpose of Ministry

I am regularly serving in a ministry.
(strongly disagree)   1   2   3   4   5   (strongly agree)

I feel effective in the ministry I'm serving in.
(strongly disagree)   1   2   3   4   5   (strongly agree)

I feel like I generally have a humble attitude that is usually expressed through servanthood to others.
(strongly disagree)   1   2   3   4   5   (strongly agree)

I've had my SHAPE interview.
(strongly disagree)   1   2   3   4   5   (strongly agree)

I feel like God has created me as a unique individual and that he has a special plan for my life.
(strongly disagree)   1   2   3   4   5   (strongly agree)

When I help others, I don't look for anything in return.
(strongly disagree)   1   2   3   4   5   (strongly agree)

My family and friends would probably consider me to be unselfish.
(strongly disagree)   1   2   3   4   5   (strongly agree)

(I've taken class 301) I have completed my SHAPE profile.
(strongly disagree)   1   2   3   4   5   (strongly agree)

If you're currently serving in a ministry, why?
If not, what's kept you from getting involved?

Write out some things that God has taught you through serving in a ministry.

What are some frustrations you've experienced as a result of serving in a ministry?

How long do you feel like you will continue in this ministry? Is it time to try something else? Or are you loving it?

Honor: The biblical purpose of Worship

I am regularly attending the Weekend Worship Service.
(strongly disagree)   1   2   3   4   5   (strongly agree)

I am consistently exposing myself to worship experiences at church.
(strongly disagree)   1   2   3   4   5   (strongly agree)

I would consider my heart to be sensitive to the things of God.
(strongly disagree)   1   2   3   4   5   (strongly agree)

I regularly express my thankfulness to God.
(strongly disagree)   1   2   3   4   5   (strongly agree)

I consistently choose God's way over the World's way.
(strongly disagree)   1   2   3   4   5   (strongly agree)

Overall, I feel like I am living a life that honors God.
(strongly disagree)   1   2   3   4   5   (strongly agree)

I feel like I have an attitude of wonder and awe toward God.
(strongly disagree)   1   2   3   4   5   (strongly agree)

People would consider me to be a person of integrity, that my words and lifestyle both reflect God's plan for my life.
(strongly disagree)   1   2   3   4   5   (strongly agree)

I feel like I have free access into God's presence that I can use at any time.
(strongly disagree)   1   2   3   4   5   (strongly agree)

Make a list of your top six priorities . . . be realistic and honest. Do you feel like these priorities are in the right order? Do you feel like you need to get rid of some . . . or add some new ones?

Name ten things that you are thankful to God for.

What are things that influence/direct/guide/control your life the most?

> WHO IS JESUS

>> **He is God.**
The high priest said to him, "I charge you under oath by the living God: Tell us if you are the Christ, the Son of God." "Yes, it is as you say," Jesus replied. Matthew 26:63-64

He became a person.
The Word [Jesus] became flesh and made his dwelling among us. John 1:14

He taught with authority.
They were amazed at his teaching, for he taught as one who had real authority—quite unlike the teachers of religious law. Mark 1:22

He healed the sick.
Jesus went throughout Galilee, teaching in their synagogues, preaching the good news of the kingdom, and healing every disease and sickness among the people. Matthew 4:23

He hung out with the outcasts.
That night Matthew invited Jesus and his disciples to be his dinner guests, along with his fellow tax collectors and many other notorious sinners. The Pharisees were indignant. "Why does your teacher eat with such scum?" they asked his disciples. Matthew 9:10-11

He got angry at the religious fakes.
How terrible it will be for you teachers of religious law and you Pharisees. Hypocrites! You are like whitewashed tombs-- beautiful on the outside but filled on the inside with dead people's bones and all sorts of impurity. Matthew 23:27

He was persecuted unfairly.
The chief priests and the whole Sanhedrin were looking for false evidence against Jesus so that they could put him to death. But they did not find any, though many false witnesses came forward. Finally two came forward. Matthew 26:59-60

He was tempted in every way.
. . . for he [Jesus] faced all of the same temptations we do . . .
Hebrews 4:15

He never made a mistake.
. . . he [Jesus] did not sin. Hebrews 4:15
But you know that he [Jesus] appeared so that he might take away our sins. And in him is no sin. 1 John 3:5

He died, rose from the dead, and continues to live to this day.
But Christ has indeed been raised from the dead, 1 Corinthians 15:20

He made it possible to have a relationship with God.
For God so loved the world that he gave his one and only Son, that whoever believes in him shall not perish but have eternal life. For God did not send his Son into the world to condemn the world, but to save the world through him. John 3:16-17

He can sympathize with our struggles.
This High Priest of ours understands our weaknesses . . . Hebrews 4:15

He loves us.
May you experience the love of Christ, though it is so great you will never fully understand it. Ephesians 3:19

Sound Good? Looking for More?
Getting to know Jesus is one of the best things you can do with your life. He WON'T let you down! He KNOWS everything about you and LOVES you more than you can imagine!

If you want to read more about who Jesus is, read the book of MARK in the New Testament portion of the Bible. If you have any questions, comments, or just want to talk, contact us! We're here to help you!

> MY THREE

>> Write down three upcoming events in your life (i.e. soccer game, award banquet, concert or other performances) that you would like me or other people in our small group to attend. I will do my best to be at one of these.

1. _____ Date _____

2. _____ Date _____

3. _____ Date _____

Print your name here

> WHAT'S YOUR DEAL?

>> We would love to get to know you! Please fill out the following questions as best as you can – no cheating – it's all about you!

What's your NAME?
What grade are you in?
Address:
City:
Zip:

Phone:
School:
E-mail:

What do you love to do?
What sports do you/would you like to PLAY?
List the two things in life that you are the most EXCITED about.
1.
2.
What are two words that DESCRIBE YOU?
1.
2.
What are two words that DESCRIBE YOUR FAMILY?
1.
2.
What is one thing that you loved about your SUMMER?
FAVORITE MUSIC (top 5):
FAVORITE MOVIES (top 5):
FAVORITE CANDY (top 2):
FAVORITE VACATION spot (top 2):
Who are the three most INFLUENTIAL PEOPLE in your life and why?
1.
2.
3.
Describe your SPIRITUAL LIFE:

List one GOAL that you have for your LIFE:

What would you like to get out of ABS this year?

What are you expecting to contribute to your SMALL GROUP this year?

Thanks!

> THREATS TO AUTHENTIC AND POWERFUL COMMUNITY

>> What follows is a fairly long list of dangers to community . . . and it's not exhaustive. Spiritual Community is tough work. Everything becomes personal. Rejections cut deeper in relationships, and superficial conversation threatens to overwhelm at any moment. Fighting the urge to be polite and nice and take no risks is like holding a tidal wave back with your bare hands.

Fortunately God's spirit is available, he is a necessary resource to create spiritual community. As you read through the list, think deeply about your relationships. The awareness of these dangers will help you connect deeply with others.

Great Dangers to Community:

1 Talking to make conversation because it's easier than risking being transparent and truthful;

2 Refusing to share our confusion and brokenness because of a critical, non-accepting environment;

3 Ignoring our personal brokenness because of pride, in spite of the fact it is everyone's condition;

4 Failing to admit our confusion, in spite of the fact that confusion leads to openness and learning;

5 In the midst of problems, asking, "What will make things better?" rather than, "What is God teaching me?" because we act as if spiritual people aren't supposed to have problems;

6 Failing to truly delight in one another because we don't look for the good placed by God in all believers;

7 Relating through unhealthy patterns, like:
    Inauthentic acceptance of one another
    Screwing around
    Accepting some, but excluding others in your group
    Offering truth without grace

8 Maintaining the status quo of safety from people rather than safety with people;

9 Operating out of selfishness, rather than servanthood.

Four keys to creating spiritual community:

Celebrate others; this leads to safety through acceptance.

See the good in others; this leads to hope through believing in others.

Discern how God is working in others; this leads to wisdom.

Give life to others in your group, so they can feel the power of Christ's touch.

> TO COACHES

>> [Reminder: Coaches oversee several small groups within a home]

Dear Coaches,

1. Thanks for all that you do! We're a little bit past the halfway mark for small groups, and things seem to be going great. God is doing some great things, and I know that I don't thank him enough for all that he's doing.

2. As you probably know, this is the time of year then things typically plateau for small groups. By now, going to small groups is a regular part of the lives of the students who are consistent, and most leaders are comfortable with their responsibilities.

Here's my warning: work hard to keep your small groups from standing still! Remember, you are responsible for creating real community that is characterized by Christ-centered relationships. Your small groups shouldn't be just another agenda item in the lives of students. It should be a place of powerful connections that continually encourages people to grow spiritually.

3. Here are a few specific areas to focus on for the next few months:

(a) Lesson Preparation: Are your leaders taking the time to really prepare for their small groups? Encourage them to use these passages as their devotional material for one day of the week.

(b) Make the most of your time. Two hours isn't a lot of time...don't let a few students disrupt the other groups. Remember, small groups are designed to meet the needs of Christians who want to connect and grow in their faith. While it's important to be sensitive to people who are not yet at this level of maturity (e.g. a non-Christian or a Christian who attends for social reasons), this program is not designed for them. Some small groups lack power and effectiveness and have an abundance of frustration because the group is trying to reach too many different kinds of people. If this doesn't make sense, please call me. Here is a common leadership myth: Can't we just help everyone grow closer to God? You can't. Not in a single location with just two hours.

(c) Ask your leaders about next-step commitments. Are they encouraging their students to do the HABITS (see page 156 in PDYM), join a ministry team, and commit to Friendship Evangelism?

(d) Mexicali is coming up soon. Encourage all small groups to sign up. The earlier, the better. If you or any of your leaders are interested in coming to Mexicali, please contact me.

Thanks again for everything you're doing! I hope this letter helps you as you coach your small groups.

Blessings,

> TO SMALL GROUP LEADERS

>> Hello small group leaders,

I love our staff meetings because it makes me aware of all the awesome things that are happening in our ministry. I thank God that he has brought together an awesome group of people who love him and like students. You are making a difference in students' lives.

We've just passed the halfway point for this school year. Congratulations on making it this far!

I wanted to take a quick moment to remind you of a few things about the small group time. There are three pillars for a healthy small group:
• Bible study
• Its application to everyday life
• Sharing

All three are important to foster growth and deepen relationships with your students. Unfortunately, not all three are easy.

I urge you not to neglect one pillar because it is difficult for you . . .
• Bible study is important so your students will learn to love the Bible on their own.
• Application is important so they have direction for their lives.
• Sharing is important so that you may know the unique needs of students.

Again, congratulations on a successful half year!

Praying for your ministry,

> TO DIVISION LEADERS

>> [At Saddleback Church, Coaches oversee Small Group Leaders, Division Leaders oversee Coaches, and the youth pastor oversees Division Leaders.]

Dear John,

Thanks a ton for all of your work this year as Division Leader! You did a phenomenal job in a very tough assignment. Apart from being flexible, you were at various times the

- Problem Solver
- Disciplinarian
- Overseer/School Principal
- Support
- Stand-in
- Organizational giant
- Sheer lover of people

These are tough roles, and you were incredible. But I especially want to thank you for the most important role that you played this year—the role of '**GODBEARER**.' In the Eastern Orthodox tradition, the term 'Godbearer' or 'theotokos' is used to describe Mary, the mother of Jesus. She is the one who, quite literally, bore God into the world through the person of Jesus Christ. Because she was available, God made himself known through her. She didn't create God, but she brought him to term and birthed him into ancient Israel. And in a very real sense, this is the role that you play.

Every time you show up to Area Bible Study Small Groups, you bear God. Every time you have a conversation with a coach, you make God known. This is what God calls us to in youth work: to become a Godbearer through whom He can enter the world again and again. Thank you for being faithful. Thank you for owning this ministry like you do. Thank you for being available to God and allowing Him to make Himself known through you.

We appreciate you! This was a GREAT year for small groups—we had over 50% of our weekend service attendees plugged into small groups! Thanks for making it happen!

The only 'business' part of this letter is this humble request: please take a look at the attached job description from last year and make any changes you think appropriate. We value your input on anything that you feel we can do with greater acuity (that means precision, but I just wanted to use the word "acuity"). Thanks!

Not only do I love working with you in this ministry, I value your friendship. I thank God for you! I'll stop now, but please know that you are loved. I pray that our partnership continues and just keeps getting better.

You play a vital role in our ministry,

> TO HOST HOMES

>> Dear Wonderful, Amazing, and Hospitable Host Home Family,

Thank you so much for being willing to facilitate the incredible ministry of Area Bible Study Small Groups by opening your home to us! Year after year we see that small groups are the backbone of this ministry. Thank you for caring about students and partnering with us!

This is just a brief letter to make sure we're keeping the communication lines open...

What we need in a host family:

We need a location that is near the desired school or neighborhood. Since we have already talked, this is a given...

The home needs to be large enough to seat (on chairs and/or floor) 20-40 bodies (both students and leaders) for a large group meeting. We can pack students in like sardines. If the group grows larger than this, we will split it and find an additional home.

The home needs to have 5-8 places where small groups can meet. This could include den, bedrooms, kitchen, dining, living, and family rooms, garage, etc. Creativity is a beautiful thing!

As a host family, the gifts of hospitality and flexibility are wonderful. The partnership between the student ministry and host home goes most smoothly when there is a working knowledge of teenage behavior... simply to eliminate surprises.

Please communicate with your coach if there are any issues that need to be addressed. Your coach will be touching base with you on a regular basis, so if there are issues, PLEASE let us know! We can't correct or change things we don't know about!

What you can expect from leaders and students:

We will work together and follow the rules of your home (i.e., no food in the living room, no shoes on carpet, etc...). Simply communicate these guidelines to your coach.

We will respect your home. Our adults will work to ensure that your home and your neighbors' homes, are treated with respect. Again, let us know if this isn't happening...

We will work to have students arrive after 6:45pm, and to be gone by 9:00 pm.

We will clean up after ourselves. Our goal is that you are happy to open your home because after we leave, it's as if we were never there!

Again, please talk to us if we are failing to achieve these goals! Our goal is a happy YOU!

Thank you so much for partnering with us in this ministry. Hundreds of lives were impacted last year through small groups, and we expect God to change even more this year!

WE APPRECIATE YOU!

> TO SMALL GROUP STUDENTS INTERESTED IN H.A.B.I.T.S.

>> One of our goals in our youth ministry is to help you develop some skills to grow spiritually on your own. Because I want to see you "win" with developing some spiritual HABITS, I wanted to give you some action steps to help you keep going:

Start with where you are "at" in your faith

Don't set unrealistic goals . . . challenge yourself without over-committing. Don't fall into the trap of comparing yourself to others, and don't be discouraged if you get a slow start.

Maybe you picked up one of the tools in the past and never did anything. That's okay, no need to beat yourself up; get started again today. It's never too late to start growing! Every weekend you can pick up any of the HABITS discipleship tools or ask your small group leader.

Discover you personal roadblocks, and avoid them at all costs

The more you work to develop your HABITS, the more you'll begin to see your roadblocks. It's important that you figure out the things that keep you from growing so that you'll know how to avoid them. The goal is to keep moving in your faith!

One of the greatest challenges in developing a spiritual HABIT is consistency, so one important question to ask is, "What do I need to cut out of my life so that I can spend time with God?"

Practice spiritual HABITS and be aware of others

Practicing spiritual HABITS will result in you knowing God better, and he'll shape you to be more like Jesus. When your life reflects Jesus—living according to God's way—people will notice the difference. It's more than just being a better person; you'll make real impact in your world!

Prepare not to be noticed by others

You may be thinking, "Wait a minute, you just wrote the opposite of this!" You're right, but, because you do these HABITS on your own, no one will see "behind the scenes" of your life. This means that not many people will walk up to you and say, "Good job, thanks for having a quiet time this morning." Some people get discouraged in developing their HABITS because no one praises them for having a quiet time (or memorizing Scripture, etc). I want you to know that God is pleased when you take time to be with him. It's a natural desire to want praise and affirmation from others—that's okay, and that's why it's important for us to be affirming of others. Just because you don't get affirmed for practicing a HABIT, don't stop practicing it!

After you have mastered one of the HABITS, I want to encourage you to move onto another one. Here's a list of the HABITS, in case you forgot:

Habit	Tool
Hang Time with God	Quiet Time devotional
Accountability with another believer	Back to Back
Bible memorization	Hidden Treasures
Involvement with the Church Body	Going to the adult services
Tithing commitment	Bank of Blessings
Study the Bible	Rootworks

If there's something your small group leader or I can do to help you keep growing in your faith, let us know!

Praying for your growth,

> TO STUDENTS INTERESTED IN SMALL GROUPS

>> What's Up?

It's that nasty time of year again, that time when summer shuts down and school opens up. No more sleeping in till 1:00 PM, eating lunch, and then returning to bed for a quick nap. No more late nights of doing (almost) anything you wanted. No more watching David Letterman because now you have a class BEFORE zero period and you have to be at school at 4:17 AM.

Cheer up, you have only nine more months. Nine months of nights filled with plenty of homework. Nine months of quizzes, final exams, tests, papers, projects, assignments, and speeches. Nine months of that daily morning growl, bed head, and bad breath; how hard can it be?

Actually, some people are ready for school. Are you? I've heard people say that their summer was boring. They couldn't wait for school to start because they wanted something to do. There's something attractive about being around a ton of people (like being at school).

The reason for this letter is to tell you about Area Bible Study Small Groups. After a summer break, we are starting up again, next Wednesday, September 17. Let me tell you why I am so excited about small groups this year:

We started the Aliso group two years ago with about 12 people. It was great! We did a Bible study, broke into small groups, and ate great cookies. At the end of last year, we had 50 people showing up for Area Bible Study Small Groups and that's just one of 20+ homes!

This year we have to use two homes. Some might be opposed to this, but we really need to launch a new home. If we don't, we will lose the purpose behind these groups. Our weekend services are too huge to get to know people in a personal and intimate way (that's okay, we want the weekend service to be a place where you feel comfortable bringing your friends). Small groups are the place where our large group becomes smaller. It's a place for where we can pray for one another, talk about the Bible, life in general, our problems . . . whatever.

I'm sending you this letter because I want to invite you to join a small group. I'd love to see you there! If you're a Christian who's looking for a Bible study and a small group, then you'll love it. There's something attractive about being around people, the Bible explains it pretty well in Ecclesiastes 4:9-12 (you might want to look it up).

Here are some details:
- The freshmen and sophomores will meet at the Bond's house.
- The juniors and seniors will meet at the Smith's house.
- Both groups start on Wednesday, September 17, from 7:00 PM to 9:00 PM.
- Directions and phone numbers are on the website.

Call me if there is anything I can do to help you.

Praying for your growth,

> THANK YOU LETTER TO SMALL GROUP LEADERS

>> Are you ready for another exciting chapter in the saga of student ministries?

I hope so! You are so very essential to the health of this crazy ministry—you will literally never know the impact that you are making in the lives of students. I do pray, however, that God would give you a small glimpse of the difference you make. Most of youth ministry is planting seeds; my prayer for you in this new year is that God would give you a glimpse of the harvest!

Here is the curriculum for the next couple of weeks. At our staff meeting on the 23rd, we will distribute curricula (don't I sound educated? It's a whole new millennium!) for the next month or so. You will also receive a tool to help you track the students in your small group: their attendance and HABITS involvement. This will make your life easier as you strive to care for students, and it will certainly help us out on the administrative end.

In this New Year, I want to challenge you to take your ABS small group to the next level. We have had a great fall season of small groups. You have spent months earning the right to be heard, so use that trust to challenge students to grow in their journey of faith.

Lastly, thank you! You know that everything you do in this ministry matters! We appreciate it, students thrive on it, and God rewards you for it! We love you!

Have a great 2nd semester of small group!

In Him,

> MAKING THE RIGHT CONNECTIONS

>> [Note: This is an outline from a weekend message]

I. Why Do People Need a Group?

1. Because we were created for relationships
"And the Lord God said, 'It is not good for the man to be alone.'"
Genesis 2:18
"Again I saw something meaningless under the sun: There was a man all alone; he had neither son nor brother." Ecclesiastes 4:7-8

2. Because groups shape our identity
"He who walks with the wise grows wise, but a companion of fools suffers harm." Proverbs 13:20

3. Because groups provide familiarity, safety, and confidence

II. How Groups Can Become Destructive

1. They look down on outsiders;

2. They don't accept new ideas, and stupidity thrives without being challenged;

3. They destroy or diminish individuality and personal responsibility.

III. How To Find People To Enhance Your Life of Purpose

1. Search for people of purpose;
"And let us not neglect our meeting together, as some people do, but encourage and warn each other." Hebrews 10:25

2. Seek to have your relationships characterized by love and servanthood;
"So now I am giving you a new commandment: Love each other. Just as I have loved you, you should love each other. Your love for one another will prove to the world that you are my disciples." John 13:34-35

"Jesus told them, 'In this world the kings and great men order their people around, and yet they are called 'friends of the people.' But among you, those who are the greatest should take the lowest rank, and the leader should be like a servant.'" Luke 22:25-26

3. Soak in the thoughts, concerns, and questions of others.
"Fools think they need no advice, but the wise listen to others."
Proverbs 12:15

One Last Thought
Nothing good happens alone! It begins with a relationship with God and is strengthened by connections with others.

"Confess your sins to each other and pray for each other so that you may be healed. The earnest prayer of a righteous person has great power and wonderful results." James 5:16

Bottom Line: you need to be connected!

> ## WHY WE DO WHAT WE DO & YOU: CONGREGATION & AREA BIBLE STUDY SMALL GROUPS

>> [Note: This is an outline from a weekend message]

Community: Those who live within a realistic driving distance to Saddleback and don't know Christ

Crowd: Those who call Saddleback Church their home and attend one of the weekend services (can be both Christians & non-Christians)

Congregation: Those who are connected to other Christians through a small group at area Bible study

Committed: Those who are in a small group and are developing the H.A.B.I.T.S. of a growing Christian

Core: Same as Committed but have discovered a ministry to serve in

The five biblical purposes at Saddleback Church
Evangelism/Reach
Worship/Honor
Fellowship/Connect
Discipleship/Grow
Ministry/Discover

Five truths about fellowship

1. Fellowship provides an opportunity **to connect** with other Christians.
"Let us do good to all people, especially to those who belong to the family of believers." Gal. 6:10

"You are a member of God's very own family...and you belong in God's household with every other Christian." Eph. 2:19

2. Fellowship provides an opportunity **to be encouraged.**
"Think of ways to encourage one another to outbursts of love and good deeds. And let us not neglect our meeting together, as some people do, but encourage... each other..." Hebrews 10:24,25"

"Two people can accomplish more than twice as much as one; they get a better return for their labor. If one person falls, the other can reach out and help. But people who are alone when they fall are in real trouble. And on a cold night, two under the same blanket can gain warmth from each other. But how can one be warm alone? A person standing alone can be attacked and defeated, but two can stand back-to-back and conquer. Three are even better, for a triple-braided cord is not easily broken." Eccl. 4:9-12

3. Fellowship provides an opportunity **to grow spiritually**.
"As iron sharpens iron, so people can improve each other." Pr. 27:17

"I mean that I want us to help each other with the faith we have. Your faith will help me, and my faith will help you." Romans 1:12

"Dear friends, if a Christian is overcome by some sin, you who are godly should gently and humbly help that person back onto the right path. And be careful not to fall into the same temptation yourself." Gal. 6:1

4. Fellowship provides an opportunity for the world to see **love in action**. (Jesus) "My prayer for all of them is that they will be on one heart and mind ... so the world will believe you sent me. I in them and you in me, all being perfected into one. Then the world will know that you sent me and will understand that you love them as much as you love me." John 17:21, 23

"By your love for one another, people will know that you are my followers." John 13:35

5. Fellowship provides an opportunity to be in **God's plan**.
"So in Christ, we who are many form one body, and each member belongs to all the others!" Rom. 12:5

"The Christian who is not committed to a group of other believers for praying, sharing, and serving, so that he/she is known, as he/she knows others, is not an obedient Christian. He/She is not in the will of God. However vocal he may be in his theology, he is not obeying the Lord." -Dr. Ray Ortland

How to get connected
"Greet the church that meets in their home."
Rom. 16:5; Acts 2:26, 8:3, 16:40, 20:20, 1 Cor. 16:19, Col. 4:15

1. Understand the purpose of a small group

2. Get plugged into a small group

3. Begin participating in the "one anothers":

Serve one another	Gal. 5:13
Accept one another	Rom 15:7
Forgive one another	Col. 3:13
Greet one another	Rom. 16:16
Bear one another's burdens	Gal. 6:2
Be devoted to one another	Rom. 12:10
Honor one another	Rom. 12:10
Teach one another	Rom 15:14
Submit to one another	Eph. 5:21
Encourage one another	1 Thess. 5:11

One of the goals of Saddleback Church is to grow larger (through evangelism) and smaller (through fellowship) at the same time.

> ### SMALL GROUP REGISTRATION CARD

>> Get Connected @ HSM!
Area Bible Study Small Groups
Starting the week of September 16th

Our 20+ Area Bible Study Small Groups make our large group smaller.
Let us help you by getting you connected! You can help us by filling
out this card.

TURN THIS IN AT THE MAIL BOX IN THE BACK!

Name:_____

Address:_____

City:_____ State:_____

Zip:_____Birth Date:_____

High School:_____

Grade:___9___10___11___12   Sex: ☐ male ☐ female

Phone:_____

Email address:_____

Check All That Apply:

☐ Last year, I went to a small group all the time and I loved it.

☐ My small group leader last year was:

☐ I'm planning on being in a small group this year.

☐ I've never been, I'm not sure what it is, give me a call and invite me.
(expect a call within a few weeks)

☐ I've never been, and I'm not interested.

> SMALL GROUP CHURCH BULLETIN COPY

>> Area Bible Study Small Groups

Weekend Worship Services are fun and energetic: there are hundreds of people, loud music, and laughter. Our Weekend Worship Services can be scary and intimidating:

• Everyone else is comfortable and I am uncomfortable.
• Everyone else is here with a friend, and I don't know anyone here.
• Everyone else is talking to someone, and I'm talking to myself.

These are some common impressions many have from our weekend service. Yet, why do people keep coming back? Relationships. People continue to attend our student ministry because they have become connected with other people in our ministry.

Area Bible Study Small Groups are the answer to making our large group smaller. It's a great place to meet other students.

We have over 20 different Area Bible Studies that meet during the week … there's a good chance that one of them meets near you.

Each Area Bible Study breaks into small groups of about 5 people after a short teaching time (where everyone is together).

Small groups are great places to talk about the Bible. We talk about the Bible and discuss how it applies to our lives. Small Groups provide an excellent opportunity for discussing the Bible, connecting with other lives, and praying for one another.

Call us and let us know if there is anything we can do to help you get plugged into a small group.

> SMALL GROUP CHURCH BULLETIN COPY 2

>> In life, there are no LONE RANGERS!
(besides, even the Lone Ranger had Tonto...)

Life is too crazy to do it alone! And there are tons of things that provide a superficial place to connect (like sports, hobbies, or music). While these things aren't bad, they don't provide genuine connections. We are glad that you are here at our Weekend Worship Service. It is great to be part of something big and exciting! However, at Saddleback, we realize how hard it is to get connected in this large group. This is one of the reasons that our **Area Bible Study Small Groups** are totally essential for your spiritual growth!

You will be known, cared for, challenged to grow, and supported as you journey through this thing called life.

Small groups are the backbone of HSM because they are where **relationships** happen! It is our dream that every student who attends our Weekend Worship Service would get plugged into a small group. In a small group, you will develop friendships with other students who live in your area and who want to deepen their spiritual life. You will interact weekly with a leader who cares about you, supports you, and challenges you in your journey.

Grab a Map!
Call the Coach!
Go ahead; they're nice!

We will do whatever it takes to help you

GET CONNECTED!

> HOST HOMES AND FAMILY FRIENDLY MINISTRY

>> Each host home is a tremendous gift from God to our student ministry. We could not facilitate all of our small groups without their hospitality. For the observers of our ministry, perception becomes their reality. How they perceive our ministry will determine their attitudes about our ministry. The following guidelines are helpful for maintaining a family-friendly respect for the host home.

1. Be finished by 9:00 p.m. Serving in a ministry is a privilege, but we don't want to burn out our leaders or our host homes. Parents also like to have their kids at home by a reasonable hour.

2. Hang out in the door or entryway to tell your students goodbye and to greet parents when they pick up their kids. Being visible is what makes you available to parents if they have any questions.

3. Try to leave the host home cleaner and in better condition than it was when you arrived. This means returning furniture to its original location. Send a crew of students through the house to pick up any Taco Bell wrappers or loose Starburst wrappers that may have been forgotten.

4. Be aware of and sensitive to any special concerns your hosts may have.

5. Be wise when it comes to physical play, wrestling, roughhousing, tag, etc. Most homes aren't constructed like a gym, so help students be wise. When the students leave, they should be reasonably quiet outside so they don't disturb the neighbors.

> FOUR KEYS FOR LEADING YOUR SMALL GROUP

>> Connections

"We loved you so much that we were delighted to share with you not only the gospel of God but our lives as well, because you had become so dear to us." 1 Thessalonians 2:8

Superficial community exists at nearly every level of our lives, and we often settle for clubs and groups and miss out on powerful relationships. Your small group should be a safe place where people feel freedom to be real and take risks in sharing their struggles. The first step to creating this environment should be taken by the leaders.

Commitment

"Not many of you should presume to be teachers, my brothers, because you know that we who teach will be judged more strictly." James 3:1

Your task is not to be taken lightly. As a mature believer, you have within you the ability to communicate God's truth. Be committed with your diligence to prepare for your small group time. Follow up on important issues.

Authenticity

"Let the word of Christ dwell in you richly as you teach and admonish one another with all wisdom, and as you sing psalms, hymns and spiritual songs with gratitude in your hearts to God." Colossians 3:16

Don't seek to offer something to your students that you don't have. Maintain a vibrant relationship with Christ. Make filling yourself up with God's Word your first priority, and then passing that along to others will require less effort, as you'll be offering directly from your heart.

Maturity

"But solid foods for the mature, who by constant use have trained themselves to distinguish good from evil." Hebrews 6:11

The ultimate goal of your investment in students' lives is to encourage them to grow closer to God. Help them mature in intimacy with God and the knowledge of the truth.

> ## HOW TO KNOW WHEN YOUR STUDENTS "GET IT"

>> Making an impact in students' lives can be discouraging, especially after weeks of Bible studies where if seems as if you're never getting through. When God's Word is taught, we know we have the Holy Spirit teaching alongside our efforts. If we know where to look, we can find glimmers of hope in our students—evidence of spiritual growth and maturity. The following list highlights some milestones that stand as evidence of understanding with students. Such a list could never be complete, but hopefully you'll be pointed in the right direction to see spiritual maturity in your students.

1. Delayed response
Sometimes a student will pause for a moment before responding to discussion questions. Students who speak quickly and "continuously" seem to be repeating something they've heard in the past. When words come slowly, this could be evidence that he or she is really struggling, and succeeding, to understand.

2. Contagious excitement
Excitement and passion explode from the learner in a way that's so powerful, it defies written description. It begins in the eyes. You'll know it when you see it—it's contagious, and it will encourage you as a teacher and/or facilitator.

3. New and different questions
You can tell that a student is beginning to "get it" when he or she asks new questions...the questions will surprise you and may be framed in a way that is personal for the one who asks.

4. Assimilation and comparison
Sometimes a student will take a new concept and assimilate or compare it with something he or she has learned in the past.

5. Personalized responses
Truth and concepts are explained in personal terms, rather than parroting back something in "churchspeak."

6. Personalized application
A student who "gets it" can quickly apply an eternal principle to a particular situation in his or her life.

The rarest of them all: clear evidence of life change.

> **PRAYER REQUEST SHEET**

Date	Person/Prayer request	Answer/Results

> SMALL GROUP PHONE BOOK

>> Name:
Address:
Email:
Phone:
Pager/Cell:

Name:
Address:
Email:
Phone:
Pager/Cell:

Name:
Address:
Email:
Phone:
Pager/Cell:

Name:
Address:
Email:
Phone:
Pager/Cell:

Name:
Address:
Email:
Phone:
Pager/Cell:

Name:
Address:
Email:
Phone:
Pager/Cell:

> SOME BASIC SMALL GROUP DOS AND DON'TS

>> **Don't be afraid of silence.**
Let the students sit for a moment and think.

Do value student input.
Do whatever it takes to affirm the comments of student input, but do not be artificial with your praise. Be delicate with answers that are clearly wrong (you probably don't want to put a big red "idiot" stamp on their forehead). Do not feel like you have to finish, complete, or correct a student's answer.

Don't feel like you have to know all the answers.
We are human, and it's good for your students to see that you are limited. You are, but most of them don't think so.

Don't read questions off the leader's guide.
Understand the questions and be prepared to ask them in your own terms. Feel free to generate your own questions during your preparation AND even on the spot.

Don't talk more than the students.
Ask questions to generate discussion, ask students to explain their answers and go into more depth. Allow multiple students to respond, even if the first person gets the "right" answer.

Do ask students if they have questions.
Encourage them to deal with the material on their own terms. Create a climate where people feel the freedom to ask any question.

Do echo some responses to your questions.
If a student's answer or comment is long-winded or unclear, repeat it back (summarize it) for clarity. This proves you are listening and it keeps the attention of the rest of the group.

Don't move to a new question too quickly.
After a student answers a question, ask, "Would anyone like to add to that?" or "Does everyone agree/disagree with that?"

Do keep the group focused and on purpose.
Don't go down a rabbit trail and leave the topics and/or Scripture passages unless something "big time" comes up (e.g., a family crisis). Be sensitive to the Spirit (but that's not an excuse to be lazy and let the group wander). Wandering is easy; being a leader isn't!

Do require and maintain confidentiality.
This allows students to open up because they feel their environment is safe. However, don't keep potentially dangerous information to yourself (e.g. abuse, suicide, destructive intentions, etc.).

Don't be discouraged.
Even if you don't have enough students for your own small group . . . we will give you phone numbers of students to call and invite to your small group.

Don't be discouraged.
When (not IF) you have a bad night. There is not a small group leader alive in the world that hasn't had bad nights.

Don't go to another small group if your small group doesn't show up.
This won't happen very often. Don't overwhelm a small group of 3 students with two leaders. Spend the small group time in prayer, writing letters, calling (phone) students, etc.

> HOW TO LISTEN WELL

>> The most essential quality that we can offer as relational ministers is the quality of listening. It is a huge value that can't be stressed enough!

Listen: to God's leading during the week.

Listening communicates care. Preparing yourselves for listening is the best prep work you can do. In fact, the better prepared you are, the better you will be able to listen (you won't have to keep thinking about what you are going to say next).

Listen: to your students by asking great questions.

Listen: to other leaders; take advantage of the support system that is in place.

> THE ART OF ASKING QUESTIONS

>> Telling someone what they need to know is seldom effective. Think back to all the pearls of wisdom you ignored from your parents... teachers... and even your pastor!

Telling someone what they need to know is ineffective for at least two reasons: a) The learner is passive and uninvolved; b) The learner may not be convinced they need the truth, and therefore the lesson doesn't "stick."

The eternal truths of God and wisdom for everyday living are too important (and complex) to reduce to a lecture of platitudes and clichés.

As a Small Group Leader, you are a teacher of God's truth. One thing you ought to continually work to master is The Art of Asking Questions.

The Benefits

A good question puts the ball in the court of the learner. Aside from generating verbal interaction, everyone can answer the question quietly and softly in the privacy of their own thoughts...when you hear a question, it's almost impossible not to think about your answer. Questions create an opportunity for your students to become active participants. Good questions allow for self discovery, as after the need is recognized by the leader, he or she seeks to fill that gap in his or her knowledge, maturity, etc. Personal understanding and ownership can be facilitated by good questions. Teach people to think for themselves!

Some Keys to Good Questions

1. Think through a series of questions. Phrase the same thing in a couple different ways. Because people think differently, at times a single truth ought to be expressed in several different ways.

2. Discern the particular truth you hope to communicate, and then create good questions to lead your group there. Good questions build on one another and lead to a particular destination.

3. Ask questions that are understandable. In our curricula, we have tried to be clear as possible. But don't settle for that! If you can say something better, then do it!

4. Use every ounce of imagination you have, and consider where your students are really "at." Use this wisdom to craft your question beforehand and to make adjustments during your small group.

5. Maintain eye contact. It's more personal and encouraging.

6. Don't settle for the "Right Answers." When someone gives you a quick answer, press them to determine confidence level—are they saying something they believe, or repeating something they've heard before. Ask them, "Ok, I hear what you're saying, but what does that really mean?"

7. Create confusion; don't shy away from things that are difficult and controversial. Don't let your students off the hook with difficult issues. Healthy confusion leads to growth. This is based upon the "Poor in Spirit" Principle: if a learner doesn't feel the need to learn, he or she won't.

8. Admit confusion. You don't know everything, so don't worry about hiding this when you're confused.

9. Be positive. According to the example set by Jesus, only hypocritical religious leaders deserve negative input...chances are you don't have too many of those in your small group.

10. Be focused. Being sensitive to the Spirit doesn't mean wandering around every spiritual truth, guided only by the tangents of your group. Rather than covering a ton of subjects on a surface level, go deep with just one or two.

11. Repeat long answers with a quick summary. When one student talks for a long time and is confusing, you'll lose the rest of your group. To bring them back in, give a quick summary, or gently ask for one.

12. Don't answer your own questions... or let other leaders answer.

13. When you ask a question, don't settle for just one answer from a single person—even if it's the "right" answer. Prompt further responses with phrases like "Good, who else...what's your take?" "Does anyone have something to add?" "Who agrees with what was said? Ok. Why?" "Who disagrees...why?"

14. Learn multiple sides of an issue. Consider common misapplications/misunderstandings/myths. This will help you create "healthy confusion" and present different angles on the same subject.

15. Be transparent. Share your inadequacies in understanding different truths.

16. Jesus commanded us to teach others to OBEY has commandments. Keep your discussions real. Head knowledge is for the classroom. You're at a small group; keep the significance of the conversation in front of your learners.

17. Learn to push things to the extremes. We often accept truths because they are nice in the few situations in which we apply them. Challenge the answers your students give you by applying them in all kinds of situations, test them for consistency, and accurately consider the implications.

18. Have students write down especially good questions and tell them to journal on them. This is also great for questions you don't have a chance to get to... but be realistic, don't dish out a dozen questions!

19. Ignite your passion. If you're never passionate when you teach God's Word, spend a day or two fasting and studying and praying. If that doesn't work, you need to talk with someone about your spiritual health, and you probably shouldn't be leading a small group.

Next to salvation, God's Word is the greatest gift we have from God. YOU GET to COMMUNICATE IT! You don't deserve it; neither do I. You aren't good enough, and neither am I. But the mystery remains: God will speak through you! Get excited about that...or get excited about letting someone else lead your group.

Excitement and passion don't mean doing back flips every week. Nor does it mean you'll always feel "up." I'm talking about the deep-rooted joy that comes from walking in the Spirit. Sometimes, I come to my Small Group tired and worn out. Don't try to fake it; if you find yourself lacking, then run to God's presence.

> SMALL GROUP ICE-BREAKERS

>> When meeting a student for the first time, there are some trigger questions that might be helpful. Beyond home, school, and grade, what does it take to get students talking? Your goal is simply to communicate care, and to get the unconnected student talking and connecting.

Following are 36 questions designed to allow good connecting conversation to happen (although it is conceivable that you could whip through all of these questions in 20 seconds with a shy freshman guy who grunts yes or no answers. Remember, he's the one who needs you the most!). Ideally, the more you're around students, the easier it will become.

If you ask a yes/no question, follow it up with another question that isn't yes/no. Example: Do you have brothers or sisters? Which one do you fight with the most? What is the tension usually about?

36 TRIGGER QUESTIONS TO SPARK CONVERSATION:

1. Hi, what is your name?
2. What school do you go to?
3. What grade are you in?
4. What do you do at school besides classes? (Clubs, cheer, band, sports?)
5. How was your week?
6. What did you do this week that was fun?
7. How long have you been attending Saddleback?
8. Do your parents come to church?
9. What do you like about church?
10. Do you have brothers or sisters?
11. Do they drive you crazy?
12. Do you have pets? Why/Why not?
13. Are you involved in a ministry?
14. Who is your small group leader?
15. What is your favorite thing to do?
16. Do you listen to music?
17. What is your favorite kind of music?
18. What is your school schedule like?
19. What is your favorite subject?
20. Do you have a favorite teacher? Why?
21. What is the silliest thing you ever did in grade school?
22. Do you drive?

23. What kind of car (or when do you get your license)?
24. Have you seen any good movies lately?
25. Do you have a job?
26. What are you saving your money for/spending your money on?
27. What is your favorite store?
28. How did you start coming here? Did someone invite you?
29. Do you have a best friend?
30. Who is it?
31. Why?
32. If you could play any sport and be great, what would you want to do?
33. Would you rather be rich or famous? Why?
34. Where is the coolest place you have ever been in your whole life? Why?
35. What do you think about this whole 'God' thing?
36. It was great talking with you...will I see you here next week?

> TEACHING DIFFERENT KINDS OF TRUTH

>> A good teacher can communicate truth well. The reality is that, just because something is true, that doesn't make it important. It is helpful to discern different "kinds" of truth. Understanding different "kinds" of truth can help you develop your skills as a teacher. Below is a passage from Mark 4:35-41. From this passage, we will draw out three "kinds" of truth we will teach.

35 That day when evening came, he said to his disciples, "Let us go over to the other side." 36 Leaving the crowd behind, they took him along, just as he was, in the boat. There were also other boats with him. 37 A furious squall came up, and the waves broke over the boat, so that it was nearly swamped. 38 Jesus was in the stern, sleeping on a cushion. The disciples woke him and said to him, "Teacher, don't you care if we drown?" 39 He got up, rebuked the wind and said to the waves, "Quiet! Be Still!" Then the wind died down and it was completely calm. 40 He said to his disciples, "Why are you so afraid? Do you still have no faith?" 41 They were terrified and asked each other, "Who is he? Even the wind and the waves obey him!" Mark 4:35-41

Historical truths ...
... are events or sequences of events which happened in the past. Although historical truths may be interesting, they do not always apply to life today, nor are they meaningful for the point you want to make.

For example: Irrelevant historical truth: Jesus slept on a cushion.

For example: Relevant historical truth: Jesus calmed the storm.

Principles ...
... are "transferable" truths which reach across time and culture.

For example: Jesus, Son of God, has absolute control over the weather.

Applications ...
... are meaningful truths which can and should be applied to every day life.

For example: If Jesus could calm the winds and the waves of the storm, imagine what he can do with the storms in your life. Trust Jesus to care for you in the midst of life's storms.

> SMALL GROUP LEADER ORIENTATION BOOKLET

>> Welcome to a new year of small groups! As you may have heard, small groups form the backbone of our ministry and are essential to its health.

Everything we do in our ministry points students to connect in a small group. It's our prayer and dream that within the small group, a student's spiritual maturity will flourish.

Our small groups exist to create a safe place for our students to connect with the Body of Christ, and to help them grow in their faith.

Powerful and life-changing community can exist, with great difficulty, because a Christ-centered environment calls for acceptance, encouragement, authenticity, and discernment.

In our world, people are quick to join clubs and form crowds, and everywhere you look, superficial relationships abound. It is our prayer that each small group becomes a "pocket of community" within our world of powerless relationships.

What you'll find inside this orientation booklet

1. What we want you to know
Important things to keep in mind

2. Who we hope you will be
Who you are in Christ

3. The small group leader cheat sheet
A summary of what it means to be a small group leader

4. Appendix
The theme verse for our small groups: 1 Thessalonians 2:8
Some "tune-up" questions you may be asked
Things we value for our small groups

What we want you to know
>Important things to keep in mind

>1. The vision and values of Area Bible Study:
>>Why We Do What We Do: Area Bible Study Small Groups
>>The Next Step: Moving Students to Spiritual Growth
>>Our Small Group Leadership Structure

>2. The Area Bible Study Small Groups Program and Curriculum

>3. Four Keys to Leading a Small Group

1. The vision and values of Area Bible Study Small Groups.

>Why we do what we do: small groups

What are we trying to accomplish?

The primary biblical purpose for small groups is fellowship (connect). Our greatest desire for Area Bible Study Small Groups is that it is a place where believing students can connect with one another and form a relationship with a significant adult. We do small groups to make our large group smaller . . . we want students to create and maintain meaningful relationships.

The secondary biblical purpose for Area Bible Study Small Groups is discipleship (grow). Every week we will study and discuss biblical passages. A portion of the small group time will be devoted to the application of biblical truths to our lives. Area Bible Study Small Groups is not a classroom (all learning), nor is it a party (all play). Area Bible Study Small Groups is a place for students to form relationships - with others and with God - so that they can grow in their faith.

The type of students we target with small groups are our "congregation" students. Congregation students are at a point in their spiritual lives where they are committed to a relationship with Christ and other believers. You may have other types of students (e.g., non-believers) show up; that's okay. Since small groups are designed for believers, chances are a non-believing student will eventually turn to Christ or drop out and attend our crowd program (the weekend service).

Understanding WHAT (connect, grow) we're trying to do, and WHO (Christians) we're trying to do it with, will help you be a better, more focused leader.

Why we have small groups

Our Weekend Worship Services are large by design. Crowds can be inviting because requirements aren't high: just show up. On the weekends, it's difficult to connect, nearly impossible to be known among hundreds. While these programs are a big part of our ministry, they cannot stand on their own to minister to the needs of students.

In our world, clubs and crowds are everywhere you look. Superficial friendships, casual interactions, and godless values make up the dominant colors in the tapestry of our culture. The Church is called to be different and marked by powerful, authentic, and Christ-centered community. We seek to create these "pockets of community" within our small groups. Here are some of the benefits for our students:

> Students can be known and accepted for who they are.
> Students can be verbal and discuss important life issues.
> Students can be accountable to a spiritual mentor and challenged to spiritually grow.
> Students can get personalized applications of biblical truths and find real help for the real problems that they face.

The Next Step: Moving Students to Spiritual Growth

You're probably familiar with the baseball diamond, our intended path for spiritual growth. Most students in a small group are congregation students, committed to a relationship with Christ and others. Within the context of your small group, we want to be continually challenging students to take the next step in their faith. The following few steps are some good places for you to encourage your students to move toward with their faith.

One next step: HABITS

We want students to develop some spiritual HABITS that will help them grow on their own. As you have no doubt experienced, there are some awesome things God does in the lives of his children when they "take a break" from life and draw near to him. Learning some classical spiritual disciplines won't just enhance our students' maturity, their growth won't be dependent on a program—they can take these HABITS with them when they graduate.

To help students, we have created some HABITS discipleship tools. These tools are free and are available at every weekend service and from your coach. It would be good for you to know what the HABITS are and to practice them in your own life so you can encourage your small group students to take the next step.

HABIT	TOOL
Hang time with God	Quiet Time Journal
Accountability with another believer	Back to Back
Bible Memorization	Hidden Treasures
Involvement with the church body	Going to "big" church
Tithing Commitment	Bank of Blessings
Study the Bible	Rootworks

Two next step: Ministry

Everyone is gifted by God—including the students in your small group! Believers who want to mature must learn to discover and express their giftedness. One of the greatest roles of a small group leader is to challenge your students to get involved in ministry. This is an important next-step in their spiritual growth! If a student is currently serving in a ministry, ask how you can help. If not, help them find one. The great thing is that you are modeling this right now . . . by serving as a small group leader.

Three next step: Friendship Evangelism

Evangelism is one of the many paradoxes we believers have created. On one hand:

- We have the greatest story ever told to share with others.
- We're empowered by the same Holy Spirit who rose Jesus from the grave.
- We get to share the wonderful joy and hope and life we received from God with others.

On the other hand:

- We don't know what to say.
- We're convinced we can't make a difference.
- We make excuses not to share the gospel.

Evangelism **is** tough. We have created the "Friendship Evangelism Challenge" to ease students into becoming evangelistic. What follows is our explanation of this challenge:

We have created the FRIENDSHIP EVANGELISM CHALLENGE to help you share the Good News with others.

First: Make a list of five friends (or people you don't know yet) who don't know Christ. Next, begin praying for your friends; ask God to provide opportunities for you to share with them about your faith.

Below are five steps you might consider taking. The first is easiest— anyone can do it. Begin to work through all five at your own pace! Don't feel like you need to do all five in a week, the important thing is that you set some goals and make progress!

Step 1: **R**eveal that you're a Christian
Step 2: **E**xtend an invitation to a weekend service
Step 3: **A**sk if it's okay to share your story
Step 4: **C**ommunicate why/how you became a Christian
Step 5: **H**elp your friend to know Christ personally

If you decide to take the Friendship Evangelism Challenge, we want to know about it, so we can pray for you.

The Bottom Line:

Within the context of the small group, we pray that our leaders will encourage their students to take the next step with their faith. Keep reading, there's more.

Four next step: Class 101,201,301,401 and Baptism

As you get to know the students in your small group, you will come to know where they are spiritually. As you put them before the Lord in prayer, he will reveal to you the specific areas and ways you can challenge your students to grow. One important aspect of being a believer is making a public confession of faith. The Bible clearly teaches that baptism is one way every believer should shout to the world, "I've been made new in Christ!" If you have believing students who haven't been baptized, encourage them to "take the plunge."

Finally, know that an easy way to see HABITS, ministry, and friendship evangelism happen is to challenge your students to take the classes: 101, 201, 301, and 401! We have student versions of the adult classes that are shorter and custom-tailored to students.

This may seem like a lot of information to remember, but in the context of small groups, you are the youth pastor. That means you are responsible for shepherding your students to grow through the four steps we've outlined.

The Area Bible Study Small Groups' Leadership Structure

We have designed three vital roles in each Area Bible Study Small Groups in order to fulfill what we want to accomplish.

Small Group Leader
An adult leader who cares/shepherds 4 to 6 students (ideally) within the context of deep relationships in a small group.

Teacher

A leader in the Area Bible Study who facilitates the "program." This person starts the night and keeps everything moving according to the schedule (sometimes this person is also the coach, and they are always a small group leader).

Coach

A leader in the ministry who is the point person for his/her Area Bible Study Small Groups. This person is responsible for the OVERALL health of all the small groups within the house. This includes (but is not limited to):

- Upholding the vision and values for the Area Bible Study Small Groups
    - Taking attendance (or making sure it gets done)
    - Overseeing the effectiveness of the Area Bible Study Small Groups
    - Holding other small group leaders accountable.

Division Leader

This person is responsible for the health of 2 or 3 Area Bible studies and small groups. He/she will occasionally show up and help the coach with whatever he/she needs.

2. The Area Bible Study Small Groups' program and curriculum

A typical night at an Area Bible Study Small Groups will look like:

Time	Action	Lasts for
6:45	Leaders arrive (promptly, of course)	5 minutes
7:00	Students arrive	15 minutes
7:15	Greeting and announcements	5 minutes
7:20	Teach Introduction	25 minutes
7:45	Break into Small Groups	45 minutes
8:30	End Small Group time, hang out, talk	30 minutes
9:00	Students go home	1 week

Although the teacher is responsible for the "program" and making the schedule happen, all leaders need to help by paying attention, keeping students quiet during the teaching time, etc.

Small Group Boundaries

It is important to define some basic boundaries for small groups to provide clarity and direction. These boundaries are guidelines and not unbreakable laws (with only one exception, see below). These boundaries will help eliminate confusion within small groups. The Coach will be responsible for applying these guidelines to his or her specific Area Bible Study Small Groups.

- Small groups will be same sex (this is the only non-negotiable).
- The best size is 3 to 5 students.
- Depending on the consistency of students attending, available leadership, and the leadership of the coach, larger small groups should "launch" another one.
- When "launching" a small group, it can be done along the lines of natural friendships, grade, or school, or arbitrary splitting can work (depending on the setup and the attitudes of the students and leaders).

The Area Bible Study Small Groups' Curriculum

Each lesson is divided into three parts:

1. Lesson preparation guide
2. Teaching guide
3. Small group leader examination guide

Part 1. You will need to cover, IN DEPTH, the first part of each lesson in order to adequately prepare for your leadership role. When your prep is complete, you'll have a familiarity with the lesson objectives and an understanding of the passages scheduled for that week's lesson.

Part 2. You will need to read through this part so there are no surprises the night of your Bible study. This final step in preparation will be to select some small group questions from this curriculum and think through the flow of your small group time. Don't feel pressured to use all of the questions, and DEFINITELY DON'T read them off the page for the first time to your group. Feel free to use your own questions. The questions are a guide to facilitate discussion.

Part 3. This section is to help you reflect on the effectiveness of your ministry. After each week, spend some time examining your heart and leadership and be open to direction from the Lord.

3. Four Keys to Leading a Small Group

Connections

"We loved you so much that we were delighted to share with you not only the gospel of God but our lives as well, because you had become so dear to us." 1 Thessalonians 2:8

Superficial community exists at nearly every level of our lives, and we often settle for clubs and groups and miss out on powerful relationships. Your small group should be a safe place where people feel the freedom to be real and take risks in sharing their struggles. The first step to creating this environment should be taken by the leaders.

Commitment

"Not many of you should presume to be teachers, my brothers, because you know that we who teach will be judged more strictly." James 3:1

Your task is not to be taken lightly. As a mature believer, you have within you the ability to communicate God's truth. Be committed with your diligence to prepare for your small group time. Follow up on important issues.

Authenticity

"Let the word of Christ dwell in you richly as you teach and admonish one another with all wisdom, and as you sing psalms, hymns and spiritual songs with gratitude in your hearts to God." Colossians 3:16

Don't seek to offer something to your students that you don't have. Maintain a vibrant relationship with Christ. Make filling yourself up with God's Word your first priority, and then passing that along to others will require less effort as you'll be offering directly from your heart.

Maturity

"But solid food is for the mature, who by constant use have trained themselves to distinguish good from evil." Hebrews 6:11

The ultimate goal of your investment in students' lives is to encourage them to grow closer to God. Help them mature in intimacy with God and the knowledge of the truth.

What we hope you will do...
Model who you are in Christ

1. Be regularly concerned about your spiritual health.

2. Be the leader GOD created you to be.

Explore the gifts God has given you
Take risks, and be ready for the difficult

3. Pray for your students and other leaders

4. Allow your Coach to care for you

You will be asked difficult questions . . . be ready to share about your ministry

The Theme Verse For Our Small Groups: 1 Thessalonians 2:8
"We loved you so much that we were delighted to share with you, not only the gospel of God, but our lives as well because you had become so dear to us."

We loved you so much ...
Ministry without a pure heart is empty: ministry must be an expression of the love in our hearts for students.

...that we were delighted ...
There is nothing wrong with feeling good because we are ministering to students. In fact, we should train ourselves to take joy in serving students.

...to share with you ...

Sharing is exactly what we are doing ... we can't force students to take what we have to offer.

...not only the gospel of God ...

Our shared gift to students is nothing less than the very gospel of God. We have the truth, and we offer the truth to students.

...but our lives as well ...

We are much more than college professors, we offer more than truth and facts. We must make large investments in relationships without worrying about the interest and return.

...because you had become so dear ...

One of the goals of small groups is for your students to become "dear" to you: know also that "becoming" is a long road paved with time.

...to us.

There are no lone rangers in a healthy youth ministry . . . remember that you are a part of a team; rely on them and be reliable.

Some "tune-up" questions you may be asked by a coach . . .

You may be asked some or all of the following things by your Coach, so that they can better care for you.

1. Is there something specific I can be praying about?

2. How is your spiritual life right now? Prayer Time? Time alone with God? Are you on an upswing or downswing?

3. How do you feel about your ministry right now?
   a. Are you enjoying your ministry?
   b. What do you like most? What do you like least?
   c. What's the hardest aspect for you about being a small group leader?

4. What's God doing in your life right now?

5. Tell me about your small group.
   a. Are you having any difficulties?
   b. How are they responding to the lessons?
   c. What are some of their struggles?
   d. Do you feel like you're connecting with the students?
   e. Have you seen anyone in your small group outside of Area Bible Study Small Groups?
   f. Are you comfortable leading your group?

6. How can I help you? Is there an area where you are struggling?

7. I've been praying for you, is there something specific I can be praying about?

8. Are you enjoying your ministry?

9. What do you like most? What do you like least?

10. What's the hardest aspect for you about being a small group leader?

11. To Coaches: Tell me about your leaders, how are they doing?

12. To SGLs: Tell me about your small group? (don't accept one word answers)

Values for small groups.

Relational Approach
  We value powerful and authentic community built on God's love and deep relationships.

Encouragement
  We value a positive environment that encourages growth, a place where God-infused potential is recognized and affirmed.

Laughter & Celebration
  We value fun; Area Bible Study Small Groups don't have to be a comedy show, but it shouldn't be a funeral either.

Acceptance
  We value a safe environment; accept people for who they are and where they're at.

Transparency
  We value real leaders: admit your confusion to some questions, share your struggles.

Involvement of students
  We value student input and involvement; they should be doing 75% of the talking, and staff 100% of the listening.

Outreach-Oriented
  We value the encouragement and development of evangelism. Pray for non-Christian friends.

Numerical Growth
  We value numerical growth . . . there are too many unconnected students who need to be connected.

Spiritual Growth
  We value our communities drawing nearer to God.

Homelike Environment
  We value the feeling of belonging; when students miss a couple of weeks, they should be noticed; when they return they should hear, "It's great to see you back."

Intimate Relationships
  We value personal relationships; these result in genuine trust.

Professional Demeanor
  We value parents' perceptions and our host home families.

Strategic Follow-Up
  We value the active pursuit in meeting special needs outside of Area Bible Study Small Groups.

> SMALL GROUP COACH ORIENTATION BOOKLET

>> [The following material on pages 174-177 contains items specific to a coach. We used the same material in the coaches' orientation as in the small group leaders' orientation. Again, the following pages are unique to coaches only.]

Welcome to a new year for Area Bible Study Small Groups! As a veteran in our ministry, you already understand the importance of these weekly Bible studies and small groups. . . So please take a second to enjoy this repetition: Small groups form the backbone of our ministry and are essential to its health.

Everything we do in our ministry points students to connect in a small group. It's our prayer and dream that within the small group each student's spiritual maturity will flourish.

In addition to being a small group leader, you have added responsibilities as the coach. You are the one who is primarily responsible for the health of your Bible study and small groups. This orientation will explain the details of what it takes to be a coach and lead your Area Bible Study Small Groups.

What You'll Find Inside

1. What we want you to know [this is different than small group leaders' orientation]
Important things to keep in mind

2. What we want you to do [this is different than small group leaders' orientation]
Specific steps to take

3. Who we hope you will be [this is same as small group leaders' orientation; therefore, it's not repeated here]
Who you are in Christ

4. The coach cheat sheet [this is different than small group leaders' orientation]
A summary of what it means to be a coach

5. Appendix [this is the same as small group leaders' orientation; therefore, it's not repeated here]
Why We DO What We Do: Area Bible Study Small Groups

Things We Value for our Area Bible Study Small Groups?
Some great "tune-up" questions

What we want you to Know
Important things to keep in mind

1. The vision and values of Area Bible Study
To fulfill the biblical purposes of fellowship (connecting) and discipleship (growing).
For students to take the next step: HABITS, ministry teams, friendship evangelism and classes 101-401.
Basic Area Bible Study Small Groups' Values
Area Bible Study Small Groups' Care Structure (coaches, teachers, small group leaders).

2. The condition of your leaders (Small Group Leaders)
Personal spirituality
Ministry effectiveness
- "You are a tune-up technician, you don't need to worry about the major overhauls."
- Learn to ask the tough questions.

3. The collective "pulse" of your Area Bible Study Small Groups
Quality control for all aspects of the Area Bible Study Small Groups:
- Regular students
- Visitors
- Small Group Leaders
- Host Home
- Parents
- Area Bible Study Small Groups program

4. What you need to communicate
- To your division leader (attendance, conflicts, concerns, etc.).
- To your leaders. Be aware of what's happening (calendar stuff, announcements, etc).

5. Who your Division Leader is . . . and what he or she does for you
The DL exists so you can be known and cared for; they are your support in the HSM.

6. What it takes to be a good small group leader
See the SGL orientation packet for further details.

What we want you to DO
Specific steps to take

Keep watch over the tone and feel of your Area Bible Study Small Groups
As the point person for your Area Bible Study Small Groups, you should have an eye on:
- Discipline
- Start and end time
- Student interaction . . . greeting
- Flow of the program
- How visitors are treated
- Are small groups connecting?
- The perceptions of your host home, parents, and neighbors

Keep watch over the quality and diligence of your leaders
a) You WILL NEED to hold them accountable to leading a good small group
- Preparation for leading their small group time
- Showing up on time, ending on time
- Doing the right things in small group
- Encouraging next step spiritual growth (HABITS, ministry friendship evangelism, classes 101-401)
- Following up on important issues and missing students
- Connecting with students outside of Area Bible Study Small Groups

b) Coach your leaders; help them become better at what they do

Seek to take your Area Bible Study Small Groups to the next level
- Are the values of Area Bible Study Small Groups being violated?
- Is your Area Bible Study Small Groups effective? Is it doing what it is designed to do?
- Are there any small groups that are too big?
- Evaluate what happens at your Area Bible Study Small Groups. Are you facing any problems?

> THE COACH CHEAT SHEET

>> The Big Picture of Being a Coach

1. Mature Believer
   Healthy spirituality

2. Pastor-Shepherd
   Encourage the broken-hearted
   Help everyone to love one another deeply
   Work hard to create authentic community
   Know the condition of your leaders and their ministry

3. Leader
   Be the POINT PERSON for your Area Bible Study Small Groups
   Understand vision and values of Area Bible Study Small Groups
   Ready to do the difficult (if need be)
   "Quality Control," help enforce Area Bible Study Small Groups vision
   Be organized and systematic with follow up

4. Communicator
   To your Division Leader and to your leaders

Things to do once a week:
- Show up to your Area Bible Study Small Groups
- Contact your DL with attendance numbers
- Pray for your leaders
- Do necessary follow up (see below)

Things to do once a month:
- Contact rookie small group leaders
- Contact at least two small group leaders outside small groups

Things to do every two months:
- Have an in-depth conversation with your leaders
- Meet with the leadership of your entire Area Bible Study Small Groups
  for fellowship and prayer (e.g. BBQ at your house, etc.) (try to
  schedule this with your DL)

Things to do before Christmas and Easter:
- Have a significant conversation with EVERY small group leader
- Write one personal letter or card to EACH leader

> ## SMALL GROUP DIVISION LEADER ORIENTATION BOOKLET

>> [The following material on pages 178-179 are items specific to a division leader. We used the same material in the division leaders' orientation as in small group leader orientation. Again, the following is unique to division leaders only.]

Welcome to a new year for Area Bible Study Small Groups! As a veteran in our ministry, you already understand the importance these weekly Bible studies hold for the HSM . . . so please take a second to enjoy this repetition: Area Bible Studies form the BACKBONE of our ministry! They are essential for the health of our ministry!

Everything we do in our ministry points students to connect in a small group. It's our prayer and dream that within the small group, spiritual maturity will flourish.

Our heart behind having you as a division leader is to care for and coach other leaders. Our adult leadership team is too big, and we need to make it small. It's vital that our division leaders feel the burden of our leaders' needs—to be known, cared for, encouraged, and helped to be made more effective.

What You'll Find Inside

1. What we want you to know (same as coach orientation)
   Important things to keep in mind

2. Who we hope you will be (same as coach and small group leader orientation)
   Who you are in Christ

3. The Division Leader Cheat sheet (unique to division leader orientation)
   A summary of what it means to be a division leader

> ## DIVISION LEADER CHEAT SHEET

>> ### The Big Picture of Division Leadership

1. Mature Believer
Healthy spiritually

2. Leader
Understand vision and values of Area Bible Study Small Groups
Ready to do the difficult (if needed)
"Quality Control" - help enforce the Area Bible Study Small Groups'
  vision
Be organized and systematic with follow up

3. Shepherd
Know the condition of your coaches
Provide encouragement and care as needed

4. Communicator
To youth pastor and to your coaches

Specific Steps to Take as a Division Leader

Things to do once a week:
• Contact your coaches via phone or email
• Contact Doug with attendance numbers
• Pray for your leaders
• Do necessary follow up (see below)

Things to do once a month:
• Have an in-depth conversation with your coaches
• Outside contact with rookie small group leaders to check up on how
  they're doing
• Visit each Area Bible Study Small Group (once)
  (you don't need to visit an Area Bible Study Small Group every week)
• Contact at least four small group leaders outside Area Bible Study
  Small Groups

Things to do every two months:
• Meet with the leadership of an entire Area Bible Study Small Group
  for fellowship and prayer (e.g. a meal at your house, etc.)

Things to do before Christmas and Easter:
• Have a significant conversation with every coach and their small
  group leaders
• Write one personal letter or card to each small group leader

We loved you so much that we were delighted to share with you not only the gospel of God but our lives as well, because you had become so dear to us.
2 Thessalonians 2:8

@Area Bible Study

Small Groups

- Be early
- Greet visitors and learn names
- Work for 1 significant conversation

@small group

- Bible Study: discuss the small group Bible passage
- Sharing: encourage personalized applications
- Prayer: pray for one another

@home

- Follow up: contact students who missed, and other special needs
- Prepare for next week's lesson
- Pray for your students

> SMALL GROUP DIVISION LEADER MEETING AGENDA

>> [At Saddleback, a division leader oversees the coaches. Coaches oversee small group leaders. We didn't have a need for division leaders for several years (when we had 10+ coaches).]

Devotional
John 21 Jesus said, "Feed my lambs." Jesus said, "Take care of my sheep." Jesus said, "Feed my sheep."

Questions
Individual home group reports (overview, numbers, general rating) Specific SGL who need help? Is follow-up happening? Do we have any leaders who we feel may be significantly slipping in their personal spirituality?

Some Current Issues
What do I do when I become aware of an abusive situation? Beware of the "lull" time: now is when groups typically plateau. New structure changes.

Goals
Weekly numbers e-mailed, SGL member lists with great info (HABITS, Class, etc) Good follow-up, HABITS talked about.

Practical
Five ideas (plus a few extra in case some are lame)
1. Don't feel the pressure to go to a house every week. Instead make personal contact with a leader or two (meal, coffee, etc...).
2. Organize the leaders to show up early to pray for their groups.
3. Have a meal with the leaders' coaches.
4. Ask difficult questions of your coaches and small group leaders.
5. Get to know all of your leaders personally.
6. Think of the encouragement you would have wanted as a SGL then do that for them.
7. Set goals with your coaches.

What are some things that are working?

Prayer

> COACH/DIVISION LEADER TASKS/QUESTIONS

>> Do you have any special concerns about any of your small group leaders?

Describe any "semi-major" conflicts you are aware of (between you and one of the staff, staff and staff, staff and a student, staff and a parent, and any other combo I can't think of)

General Administrative Feedback:
- At any of your home groups, do you have too many leaders or not enough?
- Do any of your home groups need to switch homes?

We need to know which students are in each small group. Please get that information from the coaches and get that to me.

Do you have any highlights that would make for a great "I Overheard" award? Please describe.

What leaders have you made an personal contact with outside of small groups and what kind of contact was that (email, meeting, phone, letter, etc)?

Is there anyone I should contact within the next month to follow up on something or encourage?

Do you need any help or direction or encouragement from me in any area relating to your ministry?

Are there any creative ideas that have been implemented at small groups and should be shared with other coaches/teachers? (follow up ideas, care ideas, teaching ideas, snacks for Matt ideas)

Is there anything I can pray for in your life, ministry, work, family, etc.?

Please provide attendance numbers.

> SMALL GROUP LEADER APPLICATION

>> Thank you for taking the time to help us know more about you. We want you to know that the following information will be confidential and shared only with appropriate pastoral staff.

General Information

Name:_____Today's date:_____

Email address:_____

Address:_____

Date of birth:_____ Phone Day:_____

Occupation:_____ Night:_____

Employer:_____

Work Status: part time   full time   student

Marital Status: single   married   divorced

Spouse name:

Education

High school:_____ Year graduated: _____

College/trade school:_____ Year graduated: _____

                    Degree:_____ Minor:_____

Other education:_____ Year graduated:_____

Personal and Spiritual History

Write a brief testimony about how you became a Christian (include date).

How would your describe you spiritual journey now?

What accountability do you currently have in your spiritual journey?

What people or experiences have been most significant in your growth as a Christian?

What do you do when you have a conflict with someone? How do you handle confrontation?

Lifestyle and Legal Concerns

Are there any special issues or concerns happening in your life right now that would have an impact in your commitment and involvement in the youth ministry? (e.g. relationships, other commitments, etc.)   yes   no
If yes, please explain:

In caring for students, we believe it is our responsibility to seek an adult staff that is able to provide healthy safe, and nurturing relationships. Please answer the following questions accordingly. Any special concerns can be discussed individual with the pastoral staff.

Are you using illegal drugs?   yes   no

Have you ever gone through treatment for alcohol or drug abuse? yes   no
If yes, please describe:

What is your view on drinking alcohol?

Have you ever been arrested and / or convicted of a crime?   yes   no
If yes, please describe:

Have you ever had sexual relations with any minor after you became an adult?
        yes   no

Have you ever been accused or convicted of any form of child abuse?   yes   no
If yes, please describe:

Have you ever been a victim of any form of child abuse?   yes   no
If yes, would you like to speak to a counselor or pastor?   yes   no
Are you willing to be fingerprinted for State Criminal Conviction Clearing?
        yes   no

Ministry

How long have you attended Saddleback Church? _____ Are you a member?   yes   no

Have you completed all of the classes (101-401)?   yes   no

List the date and activities of other ministry experiences here at Saddleback Church, and the reasons for ending that ministry.

DATE STATED	MINISTRY / ACTIVITY	DATE ENDED	REASON

Describe any other ministry / church experience you have been involved with.

What spiritual gifts do you feel you have, and how would you like to use them in youth ministry?

Why do you want to do youth ministry?

What are some of your expectations of the youth ministry staff?

The information contained in this application is correct to the best of my knowledge. I, undersigned, give my authorization to Saddleback Valley Community Church or its representatives to release any and all records or information relating to working with minors. Saddleback Church may contact my references and appropriate government agencies as deemed necessary in order to verify my suitability as a youth worker. I understand that the personal information in this application will be held confidential by the professional Church staff.

signature: _____ today's date: _____

Further instructions:

Thanks for taking the time to complete this application. Please give the following three references to people who know you well enough to vouch for your character as a minister in our church. Once they have completed their reference, have them mail it in to the church (the address is on the bottom of each reference form). You may want to give them an envelope that is already stamped!

> SMALL GROUP LEADER MINISTRY REFERENCE

_____ is applying to become a volunteer youth worker with the junior high ministry at Saddleback Church and has given your name as a personal reference.

This staff position is in close contact with students and we want to ensure that these relationships are healthy ones. Please complete the form below and use the enclosed envelopes to send us your evaluation of this person's character and integrity. Your response will remain confidential.

1. Describe your relationship with this person:

2. How long have you known this person? _____ years

Please use the following scale to respond to questions 3 thru 8:
1 - low   2 - below average   3 - average   4 - very good   5 - excellent

How would you rate his/her ability at the following:

3. Involvement in peer relationships? _____

4. Emotional maturity? _____

5. Resolving conflict? _____

6. Following through with commitments?   _____

7. Ability to relate to students?   _____

8. Spiritual maturity? _____

9. Ability to be a team player? _____

10. Willing to learn new things?   _____

11. What are this applicant's greatest strengths?

12. Do you have any concerns regarding this person working with students?

Thank you for taking the time to fill this out. If you have any questions regarding this reference, please call us. Once you have completed this reference, please mail this to:
Saddleback Church
Student Ministry
1 Saddleback Parkway
Lake Forest, CA, 92630

Name:

Today's Date:

Email Address:

Phone:

> ## SMALL GROUP LEADER EVALUATION

>> Name: _____ Date: _____

Respond to each question by circling the appropriate number.

1. I feel confident and enjoy leading my small group.

| 1 | 2 | 3 | 4 | 5 | 6 | 7 | 8 |

Help!   Awesome!

2. I have built good relationships with the students in my group.

| 1 | 2 | 3 | 4 | 5 | 6 | 7 | 8 |

Help!   Awesome!

3. I am available for my small group outside of small group time.

| 1 | 2 | 3 | 4 | 5 | 6 | 7 | 8 |

Help!   Awesome!

4. My relationship with God is growing daily.

| 1 | 2 | 3 | 4 | 5 | 6 | 7 | 8 |

Help!   Awesome!

5. I feel cared for by my coach.

| 1 | 2 | 3 | 4 | 5 | 6 | 7 | 8 |

Help!   Awesome!

6. I feel appreciated and encouraged by the student ministry staff.

| 1 | 2 | 3 | 4 | 5 | 6 | 7 | 8 |

Help!   Awesome!

7. The best part about being a small group leader is...

8. Things I would like help with next year:

9. I need prayer in this area of my life:

10. Next year I'd like my involvement to be this role:

> MINISTRY RESOURCE LIST

>> [This is given to Small Group Leaders at Saddleback Church. Youth workers reading this resource book can get all these materials at www.simplyyouthministry.com]

What follows is a list of books, tools, tapes. etc. that are available to help resource your ministry to students. You can get most of these at tent 3 on the weekends. If you can think of something you would like to add to this list, let us know.

One Minute Bible
This devotional Bible is a great tool for getting students into God's Word. With just a minute a day, you can get a taste of every major passage in the Bible in just one year. (cost: $10)

Student LIFE Application Bible
This New Living Translation edition of the Bible is specifically designed for students. It contains life application notes which explain difficult passages and challenging life applications of God's truth. (cost: $10)

Purpose Driven Youth Ministry
Read Doug's book that explains the foundations of our ministry! (Free for volunteer staff).

Touchpoints For Students
This topical devotional will help you discover God's answers for your daily needs. (cost: free)

Fresh Start
This devotional booklet AND journal is great for new believers, or for believers who want to brush up on some of the basics of being a Christian. (cost: free)

When My Spirituality Gets Stuck in a Rut
This brochure uncovers some principles for climbing out of that Spiritual Rut every believer eventually falls into. (cost: free)

Living On Purpose
These self-led Bible studies will help you dig deeper and get a more personal understanding the five biblical purposes. (cost: free)

HABITS Discipleship Tools

One of our goals is to help committed students develop HABITS necessary for continual spiritual growth. We've identified these habits and created some tools to help you develop these habits.

(habit)	(tool)
Hang time with God	Quiet Time Journal
Accountability	Back to Back
Bible memorization	Hidden Treasures
Involvement with the church body	Going to "big" church
Tithing commitment	Bank of Blessings
Study the Bible	Rootworks

Free Ride

Our own HIGH SCHOOL SINGERS produced this worship CD! (Cost: $5)

More than A Carpenter

This apologetic book by Josh McDowell will equip you to share your faith with confidence. In this book, McDowell explores some of the compelling evidences for Christianity in a SHORT, easy to read manner. The chapters are short! Pick this book up! (cost: $5)

The 2nd Greatest Story Ever Told

Everyone has a story, are you ready to share yours? This self-guided tool will help you create and articulate your testimony. While we'd love for you to share your testimony at a weekend service, just because you pick one up doesn't mean you have to! Working through this booklet will also help you think through the great things God has done in your life, so you can be thankful and share that with others. (cost: free)

MESSAGE TAPES: served up fresh to order

You can order any of Doug's weekend messages, we have some tapes "in stock," but if you want something we don't have, we'll copy it for you by the next week. Fill out a tape order form and turn it in at the back. (cost: $1 per tape)

Pain Hurts, God Heals

Sometimes life isn't "fair" and we find ourselves in the midst of a storm. In this 8 week series, Doug talks about the healing power of God in the midst of pain. This series is great for those of us who are enduring crisis or know someone who is. (cost: $1 per tape)

The pages in Part 2: Practical Tools and Resources, are included on the CD-ROM in two formats. There are PDF files which present the pages exactly as they appear in this notebook. These files can not be edited. The other format is in Word and can be edited and customized to fit your ministry. Also, several PowerPoint slides (included in a single presentation) can be used for promoting small groups.

Feel free to make as many copies as you want within your local church. We ask that you do not publish any of this material or post it on the Internet. Thank you for respecting this request.

If you have any questions, please call our office at 1-866-9-simply or visit our web site: www.simplyyouthministry.com for more resources to help save you time and simplify your ministry.